SUBVERSIVE CHAMPAGNE

Beyond genre in
The Avengers
(The Emma Peel Era)

by Rodney Marshall

© 2014 Rodney Marshall, Out There Publications. All rights reserved.

Subversive Champagne offers close readings of specific *Avengers* episodes. It employs critical terms but it is not an academic study. It does not engage with existing studies about 1960s television, or compare *The Avengers* with 'rival' shows such as *The Saint*. It is about the individual 'films' themselves, written for fellow fans of this cult television drama.

Some of the material contained in this book can also be found in *Bright Horizons* and *Mrs. Peel, We're Needed*, part of the five volume *The Avengers on Film* book series.

About the author:

Rodney Marshall is the son of *Avengers* script-writer Roger Marshall. He has produced seven books about this iconic 1960s television drama: *Subversive Champagne*, a study of the Emma Peel era; *Adventure & Comic Strip: Exploring Tara King's The Avengers*; *Making It New? A reappraisal of The New Avengers*; *Bright Horizons* (editor), a critical exploration of the monochrome Emma Peel season; *Mrs Peel, We're Needed* (editor), an exploration of the colour Emma Peel season; *Anticlockwise* (editor), examining the Tara King era; and *Avengerland Regained* (joint-editor), evaluating *The New Avengers*. He has written critical guides to the BBC's space opera *Blake's 7* and the 1980s Granada TV series *Travelling Man* in addition to the first full-length study of Ian Rankin's *Inspector Rebus* novels, *Blurred Boundaries*. He is currently co-writing a series of books on ITC series of the 1960s and 1970s, beginning with *Man in a Suitcase*. He lives in Suffolk and South West France.

Books published:

Blurred Boundaries: *Rankin's Rebus*
Wolf's Hook
The Walled Garden
Blake's 7: A Critical Guide to Series 1-4
Travelling Man: A Critical Guide

Subversive Champagne: *Beyond Genre in The Avengers*
Adventure & Comic Strip: *Exploring Tara King's The Avengers*
Making It New? *A reappraisal of The New Avengers*

As editor:

Bright Horizons: *The Monochrome World of Emma Peel*
Mrs. Peel, We're Needed: *The Technicolor World of Emma Peel*
Anticlockwise: *The Psychedelic World of Tara King*
Avengerland Regained: *Reappraising The New Avengers*
Avengerland Revisited: *A Thematic Guide*

This book is dedicated to my father, Roger Marshall, who wrote 15 episodes of *The Avengers* between Seasons 2-5 and created the extraordinary, iconic *Avengers* script, *The Hour That Never Was*

It is also dedicated to David K Smith who created the wonderful encyclopaedic website *The Avengers Forever!* You re-ignited my love for the series and, through our trans-Atlantic correspondence, encouraged me to write about it. In many ways *Subversive Champagne* began with the following, inspirational words found on the website:

"While *The Avengers* is clearly lightweight fantasy with comic overtones, there are also occasional undercurrents of serious dramatic tension."

My thanks to Jaz Wiseman for the original cover and to Jaz and the *Optimum Releasing* team for all they have done to preserve *The Avengers'* history before it (irretrievably) disappeared. Future generations will be as grateful as we are.

My thanks to Alan Hayes for his wonderfully positive review of the first edition of *Subversive Champagne* and for all his 'virtual' work keeping *The Avengers* out there on the World Wide Web.

"There's nothing straight in *The Avengers*"
(Brian Clemens, Optimum Classic/Studio Canal DVD commentary of
The Town of No Return)

Emma Peel: You diabolical mastermind!
(*A Surfeit of H$_2$0*)

Minister: Kill the earthworm, Steed, and ultimately you kill everything. Soil…birds…animals…Man!
Steed: Fantastic!
(*Silent Dust*)

CONTENTS

Preface (Page 10-11)

Monochrome Introduction (12-19)

Mandrake (20-27)

The Town of No Return (28-38)

The Murder Market (39-45)

The Master Minds (46-51)

Dial A Deadly Number (52-56)

Death at Bargain Prices (57-61)

Too Many Christmas Trees (62-68)

The Cybernauts (69-73)

The Gravediggers (74-78)

Room Without A View (79-86)

A Surfeit of H_2O (87-92)

Man-Eater of Surrey Green (93-99)

Silent Dust (100-106)

The Hour That Never Was (107-113)

Castle De'ath (114-119)

The Danger Makers (120-125)

What the Butler Saw (126-135)

The House That Jack Built (136-141)

Honey for the Prince (142-146)

Emma Peel 'in colour' (147-153)

Epic (154-158)

Something Nasty in the Nursery (159-166)

The Joker (167-172)

Who's Who??? (173-178)

Death's Door (179-183)

You Have Just Been Murdered (184-190)

Murdersville (191-196)

Conclusion (197-202)
Bibliography (203)
Production Timeframes (204-207)
A Surfeit of Questions/A Paucity of Answers (208-209)

PREFACE TO THE 2014 EDITION

The first edition of *Subversive Champagne* focused solely on eleven episodes from *The Avengers*' Season 4, the (monochrome) first filmed season. In that edition I described it as a major crossroads in the series. Caught between the previous season's stricture of 'live' video tape and the 'glorious Technicolor' of Season 5, film allowed *The Avengers* the freedom to experiment – visually, thematically and geographically – in new, exciting ways. I also argued that the monochrome Emma Peel era represented the artistic pinnacle of the show, when it was at its freshest and where there was more creative vitality and variety. In addition, black and white provided a noirish, clean-cut look, a purity which was lost in colour. In Brian Clemens' words, black and white was "more real" (cited on the *Optimum Classic/Studio Canal* DVD commentary of *The Town of No Return*).

On publishing the book, I was aware that I had left my exploration of *The Avengers*' Emma Peel era unfinished. The wonderful, wacky, colourised world of *The Avengers* continued to experiment and innovate, although the quality of the finished product was far more uneven. What was lost? What was gained? How did *The Avengers* 'in colour' match up to the previous season? In expanding *Subversive Champagne* a few months later, I wanted to explore a (smaller) selection of films from Season 5. By bringing both filmed seasons together, it allows us to evaluate the televisual experience which the filmed Peel-era *Avengers* offered its viewers. My original introduction remains largely unchanged and the chapters on the colour season have their own, much shorter introduction. After all, although the colour era of the series was a new beginning it did not represent a radical break from the past. As was the case throughout *The Avengers*' history, it was evolution, not revolution.

In updating and expanding *Subversive Champagne* for a second and final time, I have also taken on board two pieces of 'positive criticism' offered on one of the French *Avengers* websites (*Le Monde des Avengers*). Whilst the reviewer, Bernard Ginez, clearly enjoyed my book, he felt that it would have been helpful to have prefaced the chapters covering the Emma Peel era with a brief look at how the Cathy Gale period laid the foundations. I agree, and have added a chapter on the late-Gale era episode *Mandrake*. Ginez also felt that it would be useful to explore some episodes which – while impressive in their own individual ways – don't necessarily offer the 'classic subversive champagne' mix. Once again, I thought that the criticism was a valid one. I have therefore added chapters on *Who's Who???* and *You Have Just Been Murdered*, as well as a number of intriguing monochrome episodes which I initially overlooked; I originally wrote these for *Bright Horizons*, a collective project covering all twenty-six episodes of Season 4, created by a broad range of *Avengers* experts and fans.

Rodney Marshall
Suffolk, UK
March 2014

MONOCHROME INTRODUCTION

Few television drama series have had as powerful a cultural impact as *The Avengers*. Exported to over 120 countries, one of the only British television shows ever to be networked at 'peak time' in the United States, it has been turned into radio drama in South Africa, a stage play in London, a big budget feature film in Hollywood and, ironically, used to sell champagne in France.

The main interest in this cultural phenomenon remains the television format and it is as fervent as ever. It retains its popularity in countries as disparate as France, Germany, USA and Argentina, where it has filled cinemas in Buenos Aires (for all-night events featuring back-to-back *Avengers* episodes). It is a safe bet that somewhere in the world today an episode is being shown on a major television channel and its iconic Laurie Johnson-era score is in constant demand, re-used as background music on a range of television programmes and commercial products.

The show has been the source and inspiration for numerous books, television documentaries, academic conventions, websites and online forums; and yet I cannot help but feel that despite this continuing fascination – bordering on obsession – with a piece of 1960s 'light entertainment', *The Avengers* remains, in many key areas, misunderstood and/or misrepresented. It is continually dumbed down by the popular media of daytime TV and chat shows, which celebrate its 'fashionable froth': the costumes, fights and eccentricity, but ignore its darker side. At the other end of the scale, it has been over-intellectualised by dry academic studies such as Toby Miller's book *The Avengers*, described by David K Smith as "intellectual analysis taken to an absurd extreme", while the French website *Le Monde des Avengers* accuses it of "giving the series pseudo-intellectual dimensions never intended by the creators." My book, on one level, attempts to find a middle path, offering thought-provoking but enjoyable and accessible analysis.

It has often been observed that *The Avengers* was not created but evolved. This is certainly true. The secret to its longevity – both at the time and since – has been its ability (or need) to constantly reinvent itself. A show which began in 1960/1 with a realistic murder scenario ended in 1969 with a surreal scene in which the main characters were launched into space in a rocket (in an aptly-named episode *Bizarre*.)

In reality, the only constants were innovative sets and directors, the defining presence of actor Patrick Macnee in the role of John Steed and the fact that the heroes were avenging crimes which involved murder. Little else connects the monochrome video-taped opening series starring Ian Hendry (as Dr. Keel) and the glossy, comic book-inspired colour film world of Seasons 5 and 6. In less than a decade *The Avengers* had evolved from gritty, noirish realism to stylish, self-conscious metafiction.

It is ironic, then, that while the key to its success has been its chameleon-like qualities, for many people *The Avengers* is defined by a static image, that of a gentleman in a Saville Row suit, bowler hat and umbrella, alongside a leather-clad female fighter. One of the most famous publicity stills – featuring Steed and Emma Peel in silhouette – reduces *The Avengers* to this fixed, simplistic image. The wonderfully vague and mysterious original title has been lost in translation, both literally and metaphorically. *The Avengers* becomes *Bowler Hat and Leather Boots* in France and *With Umbrella, Charm and Bowler* in Germany; a show which was unwilling (or unable) to stand still is thus portrayed as a still-life group of aesthetic objects.

This image may help to sell the show but it masks the series' complexities and constantly shifting boundaries. From the Cathy Gale era onwards there is a fascinating interplay taking place in the very best episodes. Potentially disturbing, dramatic undercurrents are cut through with surreal, playful, eccentric elements; spy-fi meets sci-fi meets spoof-fi; the 1960s cultural context of the Cold War, sexual politics and advancing technology are seen through a prism which sometimes draws on the work of Hitchcock, can border on the Pinteresque and, occasionally, prefigures Monty Python. Paradoxically, *The Avengers* was also highly original and groundbreaking in its mid-1960s format.

My study does not explore the factual history of the show, which has been admirably covered (and uncovered) by others. Instead, in this first section, it offers a critical analysis of the late-Gale Season 3 episode *Mandrake*, followed by an exploration of episodes selected from a single season, examining these in detail, assessing the ways in which, at its best, *The Avengers* defies genre labelling. It was, on one level, a product of its time, exploring a decade that took its audience/consumers from the end of a 1950s period of drab post-war austerity, through the countercultural world of the 1960s, to the eve of the 1970s, a decade where (arguably) the taste for revolution was left behind. The Dankworth and Johnson theme tunes, though only a few years apart, belong to very different eras; both the show and the social context were radically changing.

The first filmed season – made from 1964 to 1966 – arguably represents *The Avengers* at its best in terms of revolutionary and innovative content, offering us an entertaining, unsettling visual/aural experience. Film freed the show in terms of locations and thematic possibilities, essentially liberating it.

This continued, to a certain extent, into the following (colour) seasons. What, for example, are we to make of the opening of Brian Clemens' *Murdersville*? A mundane conversation (about the weather) takes place between two villagers outside their 'idyllic' local pub as they casually watch an assassination just a few feet from their dominoes board.

This was a show with the ability to amuse and disturb simultaneously. However, by 1967 there was a tendency to veer towards a psychedelic, colourised *Avengerland* in which subtlety and wit were often replaced by a cartoonish self-referentiality. It was visually stunning but had, I would argue, lost some of its more subtle touches and innovative zest. The decision to rework (or simply repackage) a number of successful episodes from previous seasons suggests that some of the earlier creative energy had been lost. (Ironically, one of the most satisfying Season 5 offerings is *The Joker*, a Cathy Gale remake.) The second section of this book covers some of the important, innovative colour episodes from the Emma Peel era.

Before then, my aim is to examine how *The Avengers*' classic season – the monochrome Emma Peel era – was continually shifting the boundaries of audience expectation – what I term its 'constant interplay' – defying both genre classification and our desire for closure and simplicity. The following chapters centre on episodes from Season 4, the era which is generally considered to be the pinnacle of the series' artistic achievement. It is in this season, at this moment of *material* transition – caught between video-tape and colour film – that *The Avengers* was arguably undergoing its most profound *stylistic* and *thematic* transitions, from mild eccentricity to something genuinely experimental.

One must be wary of simplistic generalisations, of course. The Peel era's ability to provide radical drama did not magically appear from nowhere; without Mrs. Gale there would have been no Mrs. Peel, for example. It can be detected in embryonic form in episodes from the earlier seasons, such as *Death of a Great Dane* and *Mandrake*, covered in my first chapter. There is also groundbreaking material in the subsequent season, including *Epic, Something Nasty in the Nursery* and *Murdersville*. I will explore these later on.

It is the monochrome Peel season which provided the show with far more variety and range than any other. On the 26 episodes, eighteen different writers and directors were used. The storylines were often at their most original, ranging from the claustrophobic studio-based worlds of *The Cybernauts, Death at Bargain Prices* and *The Murder Market* – with one foot still in the show's video-taped era – to the wonderfully agoraphobic settings of *The Hour That Never Was* and *Silent Dust*. Others combined glorious sets with memorable outdoor locations, such as *The Town of No Return, A Surfeit of H_2O, The Danger Makers* and *The House That Jack Built*. Once again, serendipity came to the show's rescue. Brian Clemens wanted *The Avengers* to be shot in 'glorious Technicolor':

Even in film, in black and white, our budgets were very, very low: under £40,000 for an episode. And we begged them, we begged them for another £3,000 per week to put them in colour, but they wouldn't do it. They had no idea what they had. We wanted to shoot in colour from day one the moment we got on 35mm film. And they said 'No, we're not gonna take that chance, that's another £3,000 per episode.' (Clemens speaking to Wheeler Winston Dixon,

The Man Who Created The Avengers: An Interview with Brian Clemens 1997 online)

The financial – rather than artistic – decision to film in black and white allowed this season to maintain a *noirish* style and atmosphere which many critics and viewers feel was lost in the final seasons. In layman terminology, *The Avengers* is arguably far 'classier' and maintains a visual purity in monochrome which would have been absent in colour. Even Clemens himself – re-watching the monochrome filmed season – has admitted that the series looks "more real" in black and white. (I return to the artistic benefits of black and white in my conclusion.)

Season 4 represents the artistic peak of the show; as *The Avengers Dossier* observes:

The Avengers at this point is consciously hip, appealing to its particular young audience, and trying to pre-empt them…The viewers wanted wit that tried to go over their heads, and above all an absolute denial of the Cold War that was spoiling their party. The Avengers fought individualistic villains more and more, and governments less. Because the audience wanted lightness and laughter, heavily researched plots faded out, and quick cartoons started to take their place. This season, in the midst of that transformation, had one foot in reality and the other in *Avengersland*, and that makes it the best of the whole lot. (*The Avengers Dossier*, p. 129)

In closing this introduction, I want to define the term *Avengerland*. Anthony McKay's informative *Guide to Avengerland* explores it in purely geographical terms but this is not what interests me here. To me it is any physical space in the series – be it on location or a studio-based set – which has one foot in the real world but one elsewhere. On the surface it might appear, from the outset, to offer a normal post-war backdrop: a train station, churchyard, City bar or country pub. However, public spaces have been emptied of normality and the mundane. *Avengerland* can take the form of an abandoned airbase, a deserted country lane or pedestrian-free London mews. We have entered a parallel universe; a seemingly timeless, two dimensional never-never land.

Sometimes *Avengerland* even promises a romanticised, green-and-pleasant land: an idyllic village, Scottish castle, punting on a lake or the excitement of a treasure or fox hunt. This sense of arcadia is never allowed to establish itself, however. It is immediately cut through by unexpected or surreal acts of violence. The emptiness, and/or lack of ordinary people, simply adds to the sense of surrealism, providing an unsettling atmosphere. *Avengerland* becomes more a state of mind than a geographical location.

Contrary to popular belief, *Avengerland* is explored – if not firmly established – in the taped seasons, through studio-created locations such as a circus, joke shop or Cornish churchyard populated with London corpses. As the series moved on to film, these unusual locations became the norm; the fantasy elements were taken to greater extremes. This heightened sense of *Avengerland* – arguably the brainchild of Brian Clemens – is carefully contrived and controlled by the writers and production team, ensuring that *The Avengers* offers us a wonderfully disconcerting, alternative Britain full of eerie locations peopled only by extraordinary characters. The mundane and the ordinary have been excluded and anything seems possible in this bizarre new land/cityscape. (In colour, *Avengerland* becomes an even stranger place as realism is left further behind, the episodes often moving towards a self-referential, playful surrealism.)

This *Avengerland* allows the show to deconstruct or blur the boundaries between realism and an absurd surrealism, between serious drama and light entertainment or comedy. It also provides the audience with a disconcerting, constantly shifting, perverse world which appears to both reinforce *and* undermine the status quo, questioning our notions of capitalism, espionage, scientific progress, 'Englishness', gender and sexuality. It is, I would suggest, a world of 'subversive champagne', a phrase used by Emma Peel in *The Murder Market* (cut from the final filmed version).

It is only by exploring a number of the episodes from this season that one gains a sense of the 'uneven evolution' which took place within this single season. By the time I reach my conclusion – after also examining the colour era – we can begin to reflect on the extent to which *The Avengers*' use of recurring thematic concerns, leitmotifs and images undermined the sexual and textual politics of the kitchen-sink drama which it had gradually broken away from.

Only then can we evaluate whether the show had the necessary substance to match its undoubted style. Was it simply froth and charm, or did it manage to be both evolutionary and revolutionary? Does it deserve its iconic status and my tag as *'subversive champagne'*?

MANDRAKE

Steed: Do a rattling trade down there, don't they?
Mrs. Gale: Not bad for a ghost village.

By the end of the Cathy Gale/video tape era, many of the themes, leitmotifs and formulaic elements at play in the monochrome film season were already in place. By examining the late-Gale episode *Mandrake* we can highlight how the foundations had been laid for the extraordinary Season 4.

The 'teaser' is an entirely realistic one, as a funeral takes place amidst driving rain in a Cornish churchyard. It would be an unremarkable scene, were it not for Hopkins' suspicious behaviour, as he spies on Steed, who has himself been spying, examining the cards attached to wreaths. *The Avengers'* interest in using churchyards and funerals as recurring leitmotifs – they appear in three of the first eight Season 4 episodes – is partly because of their chillingly atmospheric settings, gothic props, and the possibility for dark humour; they are also used to highlight how people (*Avengers* characters in particular!) are close to death while seemingly in the midst of life. This is highlighted as the graveyard scene moves directly into a close-up of a skeleton in Dr. Macombie's surgery.

As Macombie and Hopkins' latest satisfied client leaves, the first sign of an unsettling surrealism is in evidence. The two men toast "Instant Death", drinking brandy with the doctor's grinning skull fore-grounded by the camera:

Macombie: The Hippocratic Oath. 'The life so short, the craft so long to learn'.
Hopkins: Let's drink to the short life.

The normal order of things has already been shaken up in this post-teaser scene: a business which offers instant death, where a doctor is paid to end life rather than save or prolong it. There is an unsettling interplay between the real and the surreal, not simply in the images, but also in the language used: their next client is described as "an aspiring widow".

The Steed we see interrogating the 'grieving' Benson on his boat in the following scene is not yet the suave, polished Steed of the film era. Here he is caught between the trench coat private eye of the Hendry era and the 'smooth' gentleman avenger of later seasons. He maintains a tougher, rougher edge in the late-Gale episodes which will have disappeared by the time Emma Peel leaves.

Macabre, black humour is another key ingredient in *The Avengers* on film. Steed's description of the recently-departed Benson Senior's relationship with his wife offers us just that:

Steed: It was a standing joke. He booked her everywhere on dicey airlines. Used to permutate for the next air disaster…If there was fog in the air, Mrs. Benson was in the air.

While Steed and Mrs. Gale discuss his taped conversation with Benson's son, Cathy is busy studying a skull, offering a playful connection with the killer doctor. (Her scientific interests and sharp intellectuality would be passed on to Emma Peel.) The skull she holds becomes even more appropriate as conversation turns to the Cornish village with its "strong appeal" for London corpses.

Cathy Gale's investigation of the churchyard allows *Mandrake* to slide further towards a surrealist infusion of the dramatic storyline. She is watched by the sexton whose closing of his gardening shears serves no purpose other than to warn us that he is dangerous. He continues to lurk within earshot as the bumbling vicar explains to Mrs. Gale about the mandrake root once found in the graveyard: "It's supposed to shriek when you touch it. Pull it up and it groans like a dying man." References to death can be found everywhere, even when Whyper tells her about the uproar when the first lighthouse was built as it would bring an end to local pickings from shipwrecks.

The macabre humour resonates as Hopkins introduces the aspiring widow, Mrs. Turner, to the vicar:

Whyper: Of course you can't tell when it'll be.
Turner: No.
Hopkins: I'd say Saturday. [*Whyper looks up*]. There or thereabouts.

The cruel humour makes way for a bizarre piece of salesmanship by the vicar who recommends a particular plot to Mrs. Turner: "Very sheltered. Gets the noon sun in winter." As the Cornish scene ends we see the sexton spying on Cathy again, before Mrs. Gale overhears Hopkins and the sexton planning her own demise. The plotting of murder, and death itself, are omnipresent, wrapped in a bizarre mixture of drama and gallows humour. Part of the latter comes from the fact that the victims are thoroughly unpleasant people: Mr. Benson hoping his wife might die in a plane crash, Mr. Turner who makes money rather than friends. Conversely, the villains are both well-dressed, educated and charming, the 'urbane' *Avengers* villain; exclusive people offering "a very exclusive service". Their witty rapport is both (literally) poisonous and yet darkly amusing:

Hopkins: Are you shopping today?
Turner: Yes, I thought I might.
Hopkins: Buy black! It'll suit you.

There is something daringly dark and subtly sinister about the master minds, a characteristic which the Peel era would pick up on and intensify, sometimes to the point of eccentric exaggeration.

The funereal humour continues into the following scene as Steed congratulates Mrs. Gale on her headstone photographs: "Not bad – for a still life." Her irritation at Steed's manner – he flicks his fingers to order up the next image – will be passed on to Mrs. Peel, even though her relationship with Steed will be a warmer, more relaxed one.

The cracker shop set offers us a fore-runner of the quirky shops and organisations which would dominate the filmed era. Strange masks and surreal, giant crackers decorate the walls. These 'guest sets' would become more and more sophisticated as the series evolved. This one, in comparison, seems quite crude, reminding us that the video-tape era episode is closer to a stage play, unlike the Peel seasons' 'films'.

As the plot thickens, Cathy Gale's description of it as "fantastic" works in both senses of the word, reminding us that the series had long since veered away from traditional, realistic fare. The Peel era's wonderfully bizarre mixture of realism/surrealism was mostly in place before *The Avengers* moved on to film. Steed's cunning mis/use of Cathy, telling her that she is booked on the evening train to Cornwall, offers a fore-echo of *The Town of No Return*, where Steed has already organised the trip down to Little Bazeley even before he asks Emma if she fancies a visit to the seaside.

The midnight fight scene in the graveyard is the one which *Mandrake* is best known for. When Cathy Gale threw professional wrestler Jackie Pallo (the sexton) into an open grave she knocked the actor/celebrity out and the incident made the front pages of the national newspapers. This tiny piece of cultural history reminds us how far the series had already come in terms of its position in 1960s popular culture. *The Avengers* was seen as hip and cool, even before Emma Peel arrived on the scene. The fight scenes were now a key part of the formula, with Gale's leather gear re-emerging, for a final season, in the Peel monochrome era. A (delayed) playfulness is in evidence as Whyper points a gun at Mrs. Gale, one which he will later confess is a water pistol confiscated in choir practice. We have been taken in by the writer, just as Cathy is duped, seeing darker drama where there is none.

The Avengers has an enjoyably sadistic habit of punishing characters who try to rise above their social station. Hopkins' financial, romantic pursuit of Mrs. Turner is destined for failure, as she warns him with her wry, dry comment about being seen "lunching with a prominent cracker-manufacturer." Her final putdown of the master mind takes place in full view of her husband's coffin:

Turner: I've traded with you, Mr. Hopkins. End of story.
Hopkins: Now I go back 'below stairs', isn't that what they call it?
Turner: Where you go, 'sweetheart', is strictly up to you!

Even among villains and murderers, there is a hierarchy to be respected in the class-bound world of *The Avengers*. Hopkins' delusions of grandeur, his over-estimation of his own worth, suggest that he will have also under-estimated the Avengers.

The next scene at the cracker shop demonstrates the late-Gale era's embryonic interest in exposing the show's artificiality. Judy is a "would-be actress", rehearsing for a part, using the set as a set. In lines cut out from the final taped version she says that she is waiting for "the end of the Kitchen Sink. The return of entertainment." Reading between the lines, the self-referential suggestion is that *The Avengers* provides just that, representing a radical break from 'kitchen sink' drama. Steed also reveals his ability to tell a story, to charm a lady with his 'painted words':

"There's this little place in Soho. It's like eating in a vineyard…Soft music. Muted corks popping. Gentle zephyrs wafting garlic through from the kitchens."

Steed is, of course, conducting business but – as he will do so increasingly on film – attempting to sell himself at the same time.

The explanation for why the Cornish graveyard has been chosen to bury the murder victims – the arsenic in the soil would heavily impregnate a body within a couple of months, making a post-mortem impossible – is held back until the final four minutes, reminding us of both the subtlety and the well-researched plots, elements which would become less prominent in the colour seasons. The final scene takes us back to the teaser, in the sense that we are watching another funeral take place. It offers a briefly cyclical feel to the episode, before Steed steps in to close the story. There is no tag scene to bring matters to a neat, 'cute' end, as there would be from now on.

Roger Marshall's beautifully-crafted script contains many of the elements we will find at play in the monochrome film season. The main difference would be the opportunity film provides to free the show from the stricture of 'live' video tape, allowing *The Avengers* freedom to explore similar themes but on a far greater scale, liberating it geographically and allowing a far more dazzling, experimental visual style. The essential foundations were already in place. Now the possibilities for the writers, actors and directors were almost boundless. As Jaz Wiseman suggests to director Don Leaver: "Because film offers you that opportunity to do something very, very different, why not exploit it?" (DVD commentary on *The House That Jack Built*, Optimum Classic/Studio Canal, 2010). In Season 4, *The Avengers* production team would certainly do so.

THE TOWN OF NO RETURN

Emma: Well, now I'm here, I think I ought to stay, don't you?
Brandon: Of course you must – now you're here – you must certainly stay.

After the stricture of 'live' video-tape, with the necessarily claustrophobic atmosphere of a studio-bound *Avengerland*, the teaser of *The Town of No Return* immediately offers us the exact opposite: seemingly deserted sand dunes, a flat landscape and a vast coastline. The sense of realism is reinforced by a fisherman (Saul) mending his nets, before the sight of a second figure emerging from the sea, in a waterproof covering, undermines it. When Brandon rips himself out, he is dressed immaculately, in a dry jacket, tie, and hat, carrying an umbrella. If the spectacle itself is surreal, then this is reinforced by Saul's lack of surprise. It is as if he has just witnessed a normal event – which in fact he has – and the banal conversation which follows about directions and the weather increases our sense of the surreal, rather than returning us to a knowable realm of normality. Brandon's warning that it "looks like rain" is both mundane yet also an example of pathetic fallacy. Little Bazeley by the sea will represent a heart of darkness for the Avengers. The appearance of the sinister title – *The Town of No Return* – provides us with a sense of foreboding.

Despite the fact that this episode was re-filmed mid-season, it represents the 'introductory' episode for the new Steed/Peel era, a fact which explains the formality of the post-teaser scene. The camera focuses in on Emma Peel's named doorbell, before moving to her Cyclops eye which opens; from the real and traditional, to the surreal and quirky in seconds. As Emma Peel takes off her fencing mask, Steed removes his bowler, a visual mirror to their earlier greeting: "Good morning, Mrs. Peel." "Good morning, Steed."

Nothing Steed says or does in this opening scene can be taken at face value. This begins with his 'statement' that he "happened to be passing by". His subsequent "friendly advice" about Emma Peel's fencing technique is playfully patronising, tempting her into the physical fencing duel which ensues, a battle which takes place while they verbally 'fence', as Mrs. Peel attempts to extract the truth behind his visit.

This scene offers us a huge amount of information about their relationship and the power games which are involved. Steed is a suave salesman, selling adventures:

"Brisk walks along the seashore, sand beneath your feet. The breeze snatching at your hair."

His reference to sandcastles hints at a childish, playful nature, while her warning that she refuses to carry his bucket and spade tells us (and Steed) that she is not going to be a subservient female partner. Her superior fencing technique allows her to overcome him effortlessly, while his ability to lure her into a trap, caught up in a curtain, reminds us that he is not someone who fights fair, despite his chivalrous/camp removal of ornaments from the fight path of the fencing duel. The fact that Emma somehow senses that Steed has already booked their adventure tells us that she knows him all too well. He is cunning, pretending to play the true 'English gentleman' but with a ruthless, "dirty" streak. The introductory nature of this scene is explained by Brian Clemens, who observes: "she's a face behind a mask. She's shown as a woman of action and when it's over she lifts the mask." (*The Town of No Return* DVD commentary, Optimum Classic/Studio Canal, 2010).

The fact that their conversation about Little Bazeley literally carries on seamlessly from Mrs. Peel's apartment into the train carriage warns us that *The Avengers* on film will both reveal and revel in its artificiality. Nothing can be taken at face value; no scene – as Brian Clemens warns us – is 'straight'.

This warning is in evidence in the train carriage, as Steed and Emma embark on a swift, witty conversation in which intertwined narratives about tea and missing agents crisscross and merge. Steed pretends to offer choice – adventure or no adventure; milk or lemon – but Mrs. Peel has no options:

Steed: Milk or lemon?
Emma: Lemon.
Steed: It'll have to be milk.

His "condensed" version of events flaunts the *Avengers* formula:

Steed: Then a few weeks later we had to send another agent to look for the first one – and a few weeks after that we had to send in another agent...
In unison: Who was looking for the agent...
Emma: Who was looking for the agent.
Steed: That's the general idea.

Diana Rigg/Emma Peel's 'canted' eye reveals her intellectual (viewer's) scepticism, as Steed magics a steaming silver teapot from his bag, alongside china teacups and Marzipan Delights; she is equally unimpressed by his familiar-sounding narrative about missing agents. She has obviously heard it all before. Their reading material, *Primary Education* for Emma, *Great Disappearing Acts* for Steed, shows us two actors/characters attempting to take on new roles. (The seamless visual transition from the steaming teapot to the train's own steam is typical of the episode's clever, playful stylishness.)

As Steed, Emma Peel and Smallwood – the passenger who has joined them – arrive at their destination, the 'Welcome to Little Bazeley' sign is immediately followed by the sight of a hostile-looking Saul, whose mad gaze is in turn replaced by the 'PEACE' sign on a graveyard stone cross, this making way for the pub sign for The Inebriated Gremlin. There are signs everywhere, all asking to be read, digested and analysed.

The quirky name and board of the seaside village pub offers a momentary flicker of hope that it will provide a warm, log fire welcome, in stark contrast to the dismal, windy weather outside, but the haunting music warns us that this is unlikely. We enter before the visitors do, and both the silence and the stern faces set the cold, unfriendly atmosphere. Steed's immediate comment "chilly is the word for it, decidedly chilly" refers to Little Bazeley inside and out.

Initially, landlord 'Piggy' Warren seems to offer the antithesis of his clientele, with his welcoming, childish public-school banter and ridiculous moustache. However, his questioning of Smallwood, Steed and Mrs. Peel borders on interrogation and his explanation of the frosty locals will turn out to be ironically false:

"Oh, they're not as bad as they look. Country folk, you know... suspicious of strangers...basically a fine bunch of chaps."

They are, of course, all strangers – enemy agents – and are acting out their stereotypical roles. The unsettling atmosphere is increased as Mark Brandon – the waterproof figure in the teaser – 'welcomes' Mrs. Peel:

Emma: Well, now I'm here, I think I ought to stay, don't you?

Brandon: Of course you must – now you're here – you must certainly stay.

We are beginning to understand why the title of this episode is *The Town of No Return*. The following scenes alternate between the almost agoraphobic feel of the coastline and the claustrophobic atmosphere of the pub. Steed is discouraged from leaving the pub to post a letter, while the exit of gun-toting locals, soon after Smallwood leaves, is explained away as "a spot of badger hunting. It's more fun at night." The sight and the explanation are ridiculous, yet they increase the dramatic tension rather than undermine it.

In the exterior scenes, the sight of Saul stalking Smallwood as dusk settles offers a series of noirish, chilling images amidst deserted windswept lanes and an empty smithy, despite the fire burning. Meanwhile, the pub bedrooms have nailed-down windows, increasing the sense of the Avengers being trapped. The close-up of an old pilot's mask provides an irrationally disturbing image, one which moves directly onto that of a skull on a parish gravestone. More signs left for us to take in and interpret if we so wish. As Smallwood approaches the church, passing the 'PEACE' sign, the hymn playing is *All Things Bright and Beautiful*, horribly at odds with the images we are viewing. The sense of surrealism peaks as Smallwood opens the church door to find a deserted interior, despite the singing and music.

The sand dunes have now become the location for a human hunt, Smallwood's ripped clothing and terrified face offering a sense of realism and surrealism interplaying. The silhouettes of Saul, the hounds and Smallwood on the horizon swap with the sight of Steed and Mrs. Peel eating unenthusiastically in front of the pub's log fire, with the 'soundtrack' of the hunt disturbing them even more than us. The final close-up of the captured, cornered Smallwood contrasts – as Clemens observes – with the vastness of the landscape.

We are twenty minutes in and yet it is only now that the investigation really gets going, reminding us of the subtlety of *The Avengers* at this stage in the show's history. Up until now, it has been a case of building up the unsettling atmosphere.

The scene in which Steed throws pebbles on the beach is a memorable one. Beginning playfully enough, the sight of a dozen pairs of feet in the sand, coming out of the sea, leads Steed to quote from *Alice in Wonderland*. The storyline, like Lewis Carroll's surreal tale, is becoming "curiouser and curiouser". As he observes, "all is not as it should be":

"I've been surveying the countryside. The tractors all stopped. Ploughs rusting in the furrows."

There is an apocalyptic feeling emerging, as if we have arrived in a post-nuclear attack landscape, mirroring the Cold War plot which will soon be unveiled. The discovery of Smallwood's body in the sand is disturbingly realistic, his broken glasses returning us to a recurring leitmotif, symbolising, perhaps, the fragility of human life in *Avengerland*. The sense of a depopulated space is at the heart of the dramatic undercurrent, as it would be in *The Hour That Never Was*: "And where have all the people gone?...I haven't seen a solitary soul."

Visually, this episode is impressively noirish and the scenes cleverly, seamlessly move into each other, the fire of the smithy becoming the log fire of the pub, playfully suggesting that both are darkly dangerous locations.

The church appears at first to offer an oasis of normality, the Reverend Jonathan Amesbury a mildly eccentric, gentle country vicar, complaining of bats in the belfry and mice in the organ. Mrs. Peel is certainly charmed, although Smallwood's earlier venture inside has warned us that nothing is as it seems.

Steed's exploration of the abandoned airbase is the episode's central scene in terms of the playful interplay of the real and surreal, the dramatic and the light-hearted, the elegiac and the chilling. Faced with a weed-strewn parade ground, Steed imagines the sounds of soldiers marching, planes flying. He even offers a salute. Next, he moves on to the playground, sitting on the merry-go-round, accompanied by fairground music. The carefree, boyish moment is a fleeting one, giving way to the real/surreal sight of a 33 Squadron door opened to reveal a concrete floor without walls or roof, rusting dormitory beds, and a broken mirror which Steed acknowledges with his bowler. The dramatic undercurrent pulses again as Steed pieces together the bricks of a crude jigsaw which records the loss of 'Piggy' Warren, killed in action in 1942. The constant, theoretical threat of the Cold War is set alongside the historical reality of World War Two.

The strange nature of the disturbing drama is mirrored by Mrs. Peel being held at gunpoint by the vicar, while a taped choir plays a requiem. *The Town of No Return*'s heightened atmosphere is reaching breaking point. Mrs. Peel's ironic smile as she is cornered by Saul, the fake Brandon and vicar promises us that the tension will be overcome. Eventually.

The final pub scene reveals Steed's ability to instantaneously transform from charming gentleman to cut-throat investigator. His interrogation of the imposter Warren is ruthless and, as 'Piggy's moustache catches fire, Steed's genuine concern about Mrs. Peel's disappearance is matched by his enjoyment of the landlord's squirming discomfort:

"You're expendable, Piggy. You're dead, remember? Killed in action 1942. Where is she, Piggy? Where is she?"

Once again, the move into the following blacksmith scene is cleverly seamless, the burning moustache replaced by a glowing, hot horseshoe. Steed's fight with Saul begins 'straight' before ending with a stylishly artificial knock-out from the reinforced bowler and the unsaddling of a tied-up Mrs. Peel who he advises needs "to cut down on the oats". Despite the increase in the action as we enter the final few minutes, there is still time for the playful, as 'schoolmistress' Peel offers Steed a lesson about the diabolical master plan as Steed sits attentively behind a child's desk, putting up his hand to make suggestions; even the formulaic explanation scene has a quirky playfulness to it in *The Town of No Return*.

The underground tunnels/bunkers scene lacks the earlier tension. It is as if the discovery of the plot is more important than the foiling of it. The protracted final fight action benefits from the wonderfully theatrical lowering of the metallic portcullis door, allowing Steed to dispose of a handful of armed soldiers before the 'curtain' rises again. It as much a fantasyland as the 'bright horizon' which Steed and Mrs. Peel head towards on a scooter in the 'tag' scene, the country lane every bit as deserted as Little Bazeley was.

The tag scenes throughout Season 4 are interesting additions. In each episode Steed and Mrs. Peel go off in a form of transport – motor bike, taxi, vintage motor car, milk float, hot air balloon, hearse, miniature train, rickshaw, tractor trailer, 'flying carpet' etc. – which are often related to the thematic content of the episode itself. Here it is a scooter, with Mrs. Peel in the driving seat, Steed uncomfortably holding on. Alongside their 'witty banter', the scriptwriters offer a (formulaic) description of them riding off "towards a bright horizon".

There is an element of audience 'comfort' or reassurance, here. The message appears to be that although we may have just watched something quite bizarre, which at times has surprised us, even made us feel uncomfortable, undermining our expectations, everything is now fine. The blurred boundaries have been redefined, 'normal service' has been restored and, of course, our heroes will be back next week. We have been taken well beyond formula, but within a formulaic structure. *The Town of No Return* offers its audience that 'constant interplay' I referred to in my introduction between an undercurrent of violence and danger and a reassurance that humour will prevail, that despite the threat of 'rain' at the outset, we will reach the 'bright horizon' at the conclusion.

The Town of No Return offers an almost faultless starting point for viewers to the adventurous, innovative, playful new world of *The Avengers* on film. Many of the character types, places and leitmotifs which would dominate over the forthcoming seasons are re/introduced. These include: grinning imposters; atmospheric, agoraphobic, deserted locations; claustrophobic, interior traps; graveyards and churches. Subtle wit, light-hearted action-adventure and a darker dramatic undercurrent combine as the plot mixes realism and surrealism, defying any desire to define – or confine – *The Avengers* within a specific genre, calling into question traditional television drama classification or labelling. There is style, charm and wit, providing the sparkling 'champagne'; there is also a darker drama, including oddly surreal, unsettling images and experimental camera work which offer us playfully 'subversive' elements.

As a postscript, it would be fascinating to unearth the original *The Town of No Return,* filmed with Elizabeth Shepherd in the co-lead role. Parts of this were used when the final version was put together. *The Town of No Return* is historically interesting, given the decision to 'release' the original Emma Peel. We are unlikely to ever see the original; it may not even remain in existence. Nevertheless, the fact that there are/were two different versions of the episode adds a further layer to this already fascinating introduction to *The Avengers* on film. *The Town of No Return* represents both a defining presence at the beginning of a new era, but also a mysterious absence.

THE MURDER MARKET

Lovejoy: With someone like yourself – well, our entire range is at your disposal.
Steed: Fascinating. Do you have a catalogue?

The 'teaser' for *The Murder Market* is one of the most memorable of the season. Unlike *The Town of No Return* – where the pre-title scene sets the surreal tone but offers us little else in the way of clues – here the dominating themes are immediately explored: dating agencies, hot-blooded (male) sexual predators and cold-blooded (female) assassins. Jonathan Stone – who will later be described by his widow as a serial womaniser – does all the speaking, employing a range of stereotypical clichés such as: "it [the photograph] doesn't do you justice" while Barbara Wakefield, the hired killer, remains ominously silent. She is described in the script as smiling "in a cold, calculating" manner, then shooting him "impassively". The traditional male/female, power/powerless oppositions are turned around, the man nervous and awkward, the woman terminating him with "three little silenced swishes" of her gun.

The surreal setting for this murder is an aquarium – deserted, of course – and both the first and the final camera shots are typically stylish. In the initial one we see Stone through the glass prism of a fish tank; the last one shows water starting to pour from "three neat holes" in the tank, confirming that he has indeed been murdered and adding an equally neat cyclical structure to the teaser. The title of the episode appears on the screen, warning us that capitalism and the desire for money will be at the heart of the plot. By setting this opening, defining scene in an aquarium we are offered a playfully intertextual, visual reference to Hitchcock's *Sabotage* and this is appropriate given the fact that another of the director's classic films is a key influence on the plot for *The Murder Market*.

The opening scenes between John Steed and Emma Peel – the first ever shot with the new actress on board – offer examples of their witty repartee, here as a form of verbal fencing. Peel's ability to size up both the nature of the case and Steed's manipulative approach to their workload is instant and her dialogue is laced with both irony and sarcasm. The scene is humorous but we empathise with Peel's discomfort, once again providing us with a sense of a television programme which is pulling its audience in a number of opposing directions.

If the 'teaser' can be seen as sexually countercultural – the female assassin sticking it in to the male predator – then the subsequent scene in the photography studio is equally interesting. Drawing on films such as *Rear Window* and *Peeping Tom*, the camera here is turning the female model into an object which, as Susan Sontag might describe it, is 'symbolically possessed'. The music, the model's fashionable tomboyish look, and Beale's demeanour perfectly capture the swinging sixties atmosphere. When Steed places his bowler hat on her head, it offers us an avengerish image. In an instant, he has changed a "mundane" photo-shoot into something more interesting or off-beat – as the photographer gratefully acknowledges – just as the series would subtly transform traditional espionage drama. The photographer's desire to find an interesting, quirky camera angle – rather than the conventional one – also mirrors the show's experimental approach.

The two scenes are, of course, intrinsically linked and share common themes, most notably 'the market'. Here, the model shoot is advertising an expensive watch, whereas Wakefield is working for the Togetherness agency which is taking money from rich clients, the sort who might buy the product being promoted by Beale's bored model. The fact that Beale's work includes portraits for Togetherness reinforces the connections between advertising, money and sex; watches and arranged weddings are commodities to be bought and sold.

Togetherness offers us a critique of dating agencies on a number of levels. Beale's final comment to Steed – offered in a playfully plummy accent – is: "Very exclusive. Only the best people – but a marriage bureau just the same." This sense of sex and love as commercial commodities is reflected in Steed's parting comment to Emma Peel before he visits it for the first time: "I offer myself on the market today. Every bid considered…"

Togetherness' motto – "Where there is always a happy ending" – (self-referentially?) mirrors *The Avengers* formula, with its obligatory tag scene. The set is typically over-the-top *Avengerland*: a shower of confetti, floating cupids and other romantic statues, cheesy floral displays, a heart-shaped reception desk and 'loveseats'. Not unlike the fake 'Piggy' Warren, Mr. Lovejoy is another of *The Avengers*' comic villains. His company not only draws on the banal commercialisation of 'love', it also offers a service which reduces the romantic quest for love to a 'scientific' formula.

The interview which takes place between Lovejoy and Steed beautifully satirises not only the commercial nature of dating agencies but also the snobbery inherent in the English class system. The fact that Steed has created a fictionalised upper-class Steed who has no need to work makes him "eminently suitable" as a Togetherness client. Lovejoy's description of the nature of the business allows Steed to poke fun at the capitalisation of sexual desire:

Lovejoy: With someone like yourself – well, our entire range is at your disposal.
Steed: Fascinating. Do you have a catalogue?

The critique of the dating agency is taken a significant step further in the parallel scene in which Lovejoy interviews Mrs. Peel. It is clear that at Togetherness the male clients are expected to provide the financial capital, while the female clients are the decorative ornaments being valued. When asked what her requirements are, Lovejoy is "taken aback" by Emma's request for a man with "stamina".

This is not the only 'parallel' scene in the episode. Steed's initial date with the female assassin cleverly replicates the teaser. The setting is the same, although this time Steed playfully responds to the initial aquarium tank camera shot by mimicking the fish. There is the identical "cold, calculating" look on Barbara Wakefield's face. When Steed uses Jonathan Stone's chat-up line – "Well er – now that you've met me, what do you think?" – and Wakefield touches her handbag, we, as viewers, are manipulated into wondering for a split-second whether Steed will be killed. The repetition of the clichéd dialogue – which on the level of realism is absurd as Steed is unaware of the earlier verbal exchange – is *The Avengers* playfully displaying its own fictionality while simultaneously raising the dramatic temperature. We are concerned for Steed, despite the ridiculous nature of the 'mirror' scene.

Earlier, I fleetingly referred to echoes of Hitchcock in the aquarium and photo studio scenes. The basic premise of Togetherness – clients swapping murders to provide cast-iron alibis – is clearly borrowed by script writer Tony Williamson from *Strangers on a Train*. *The Avengers* shares a Hitchcockian sense of self-referentiality and a dark, occasionally sadistic, humour. This is highlighted in a scene between Steed and Emma after Steed has been ordered to murder his fellow Avenger. He opens a bottle of champagne, enigmatically referring to it as "a sort of farewell gesture". The scene ends with the following piece of dialogue:

Emma: Steed…! Who are you supposed to kill?
Steed: You, my dear.

We are left with the image of Steed pointing a gun at Mrs. Peel and, despite the viewer knowing – in the rational sense – that he will not commit the crime – our irrational sense of fear and horror once again take over. We are being toyed with, as so often in this season.

Earlier in the scene, Mrs. Peel refers to Steed's "subversive champagne" – cut in the final filmed version – and this is an apt description of the effect which the season and series offer, at their very best: despite the enjoyable froth, there is a constant interplay between light-hearted humour and a disturbing undercurrent, demonstrated when Steed and Lovejoy admire the "peaceful" Mrs. Peel as she lies on display in a coffin. Steed offers the hope that "her past sins – there were many from what I can gather – will be overlooked". Is this mischievous remark meant to tease, amuse or infuriate her? After all, she cannot be dead, can she? Subversive champagne also refers to John Steed at the beginning of the *Avengers* film era: he has charm and wit bubbling out of him but still retains a darker, more subversive edge which (unfortunately) disappears in colour.

The humour of the following champagne-guzzling coffin scene has been tainted in advance as we now know that Emma Peel is to be buried alive, with Steed an (unwilling) accomplice to the crime. The sense of the show's 'subversive champagne' is at its most powerful in moments such as this.

There is a darkly playful symmetry as Mrs. Peel's eyes dramatically open just as the coffin lid shuts. It is also darkly ironic that the funeral scene is the only time when we escape the claustrophobic studio-bound world in this episode. Rather than releasing or liberating the viewer, it intensifies the sense of stricture.

If the Steed-designed coffin – "a lead floor to give it weight...and a hinged side to give an emergency exit" – reminds us of James Bond gadgets, the ending is pure *Avengers*, with the final fight scene taking us into a reassuringly silly scenario. As the battle takes place, banal wedding accessories, cakes and floral displays are used as weapons and missiles, knocked-out baddies roll into artistically-stylish resting places and confetti is scattered on the bodies. Any sense of subversion has given way to the comfort of the 'happy ending' and an amusing tag scene in a hearse.

Once again, though, we have experienced something disconcerting: an episode which asks us to question the increasing commercialisation of romance, the worryingly 'scientific' (computerised) approach to relationships. It is not just people who are murdered in this episode. Marriage as a symbol of love is shattered; it is portrayed as a cold, loveless commodity or market, run by a woman called Stone, with a heart to match.

The Murder Market is not a feminist text; it is not even an anti-male story. Instead, it asks questions about a world in which it is socially acceptable to be unemployed, as long as you are the 'right' sort of person, where 'love' is to be found through computer profiling rather than social interaction, and where both murder and marriage have a price which is agreed by financial contracts.

THE MASTER MINDS

Steed: There is a kind of fantasy about it all, isn't there?

The Master Minds has a playfully self-referential title, poking fun at the formulaic approach of a series in which Steed and his female partner encounter diabolical masterminds on a weekly basis. The teaser, once again, plunges us immediately into a strange world where the realism of a burglary is undercut by the strange guards' uniforms which the criminals are wearing. The director offers us a daringly effective camera angle as the security gate descends, threatening to squash one of the robbers and the camera itself. The decision to terminate the bungling burglar – the leader of the gang chillingly ordering another man to "Kill him!" – heightens the tension.

The post-teaser scene demonstrates how simply *The Avengers* on film creates an effective sense of atmosphere. Steed's car heads along deserted country lanes against a backdrop of bare winter trees, the fore-grounded milk churns – as much as the blazing headlamps and the half-light – telling us that it is dawn. If a sense of realism has emerged then this is not allowed to establish itself as Sir Clive Todd's elderly butler answers the door in a surgeon's mask. The Sixties interior – with a central, circular brick fireplace – is undermined by the odd sight of the same, 'timeless' uniform we saw in the teaser:

Emma: Steed, you did wake me up a few minutes ago?
Steed: There is a kind of fantasy about it all, isn't there? Toy soldiers, and all that.
Emma: Is it some kind of fancy dress party?

There is a deliciously artificial layer here. The Avengers are talking as much about the series in general as they are about Sir Clive Todd's odd choice of clothes. As if to emphasise this, the plot pauses while the camera focuses in on Mrs. Peel, taking her in from head to toe as she shows off the glamorous outfit which has remained hidden underneath her coat. As Jaz Wiseman observes on the Optimum DVD commentary, the setting and fashions "encapsulate the whole Swinging Sixties feel"; the scriptwriter Robert Banks Stewart remarking that: "The Swinging Sixties were very, very fully represented by the filmed series of *The Avengers*." This self-consciously staged 'fashion shoot' moment will be playfully echoed later when Sir Clive's daughter Davinia reveals the Côte d'Azur bikini underneath her leopard-skin coat, offering an image of the more countercultural, permissive side of the decade with its sexual revolution, something which the cutting-edge, subversively sexy Emma Peel was at the heart of.

The appearance of Campbell, a Service Psychiatrist, brings with it another battle between realism and something more playfully bizarre. Seemingly forgetting that Sir Clive is the patient, he offers a snap judgement of Steed: "Your facetiousness covers an edgy temperament...I'd say your nerves mostly jangle like wires in the wind." The bedside consultation becomes confrontation in the form of verbal jousting, with Steed able to arm himself with the required psycho-babble: "Traces of an incipient inferiority complex. I should watch it!" With his ability to put people down through witty retorts, it is little wonder that Steed rarely carries a gun in this season. These opening ten minutes demonstrate the innovatively daring internal conflict at play in *Avengers* episodes in terms of genre and style.

Despite the slick, stylish opening, *The Master Minds* is best remembered for its 'second half', set at an all-girls' boarding school. Our introduction to the 'college for young ladies' comes immediately after the 'straight' scenes in which Steed tries to understand why the psychiatrist has (reluctantly) murdered Sir

Clive. Our first sight of the notice-board breaks the previous dramatic tension, the school motto – 'Defend Thy Honour' – almost tailor-made for Steed, both in terms of his avengering and his pursuit of the opposite sex. The humour continues to dominate as Steed encounters 'eggheads' in the midst of ridiculously cerebral conversations, playfully poking fun at the early 1960s fashion for MENSA's intellectual elitism and perceived snobbery. When Steed encounters Professor Spencer standing on his head in the gymnasium, the absurdity of the image is increased by the camera work, offering us the Professor's viewpoint, with Steed now (seemingly) upside down. This is a perfect example of the season's desire to disorientate or challenge the viewer, providing us with disconcerting yet excitingly new artful approaches to television drama. Steed – our avengering hero – is reduced to a cheating schoolboy as he crouches over a tiny desk, sitting the RANSACK IQ test, relying on stealth, and the far more intellectual Emma Peel, in order to win favour from the organisation. The playfulness continues as Steed explores his temporary bedroom. Opening the wardrobe, he discovers a girl's gallery of bare-chested musclemen, flexing his own for comparison, before smiling wryly at the sign, 'If you can't sleep, ring for a mistress.'

We sense that the leisured humour or 'champagne' will soon be undercut, in turn, by a darker drama. The strange, eerie music score helps to create the sense of disquieting mystery as Steed watches the other RANSACK members making their way downstairs like zombies. This strange scene will repeat itself, both increasing Steed and our own sense of bewilderment but also adding a further cyclical or labyrinthine feel to the story, as if Steed is caught up in a puzzling intellectual maze. The camera initially provides us with Steed's eye-view as he watches the hypnotised members staring ahead in the gym, the flickering shadows which appear on their faces telling us and him that they are watching a film. It is this type of stylish shot which provides *The Avengers* with its champagne sparkle.

Robert Banks Stewart's description of the mixture of "thrill and comedy" (Optimum/Studio Canal DVD commentary) in *The Avengers*' plots matches, to a certain extent, my own use of 'subversive champagne' to describe the fascinating interplay between different genres and styles which collide in *The Master Minds*, as elsewhere in Season 4. Jaz Wiseman describes it as "magic dust" which is being "sprinkled" on a 1960s television drama which would otherwise simply have been yet another formulaic espionage series.

The darkest moment of *The Master Minds* occurs as Steed has finally been uncovered as a spy and Mrs. Peel – who we think is still under a hypnotic trance – volunteers to kill him on the moonlit archery range. The scene is superbly structured as we constantly switch between Emma Peel's silhouetted figure in the distance, preparing to fire an arrow at Steed, and the latter's close-up face in front of the target, as uncertainty changes to disbelief and fear. When the camera finally closes in on Emma she fires, and smiles. We are left uncertain as to where her arrow has landed. The scene is stylish, disturbing and beautifully shot.

This begins a playful final ten minutes in which we are teased by the script on a number of levels. The villains are aware that she is no longer in a state of trance and *The Master Minds* finally moves from atmosphere into action. Steed – like an urban Tarzan – swings in on Professor Spencer's rope which we should have guessed would be playfully redeployed. The fight finale is delightfully surreal, as the real tussle takes place directly in front of the mastermind's film which shows military personnel heading into action of their own. The double spectacle acts on a playfully self-referential level before becoming surreal as the silhouettes of Emma Peel and the (still unknown) mastermind fight behind the projection screen. As Wiseman remarks, it is "such an *Avengers* touch". As the villains' film is sent into reverse so are their plans. How fitting that the cliché of the unmasking is countered by the manner, as the games mistress is sent tumbling through the projection canvas, landing at Steed's feet. The diabolical plan, the dramatic action and the surreal image have all been literally ripped apart.

If I have a reservation about *The Master Minds* it is simply that it feels like two episodes, one set at Sir Clive's home, the other at the boarding school, rather than an organic whole. If the first offers us the Sixties feel of the season, the second provides us with a stylish surrealism. However, both parts offer us plenty of subversive champagne as we are encouraged to forget about the weapons plot and simply enjoy the spectacle.

DIAL A DEADLY NUMBER

Harvey: Do you like wine, Mrs. Peel?
Emma: In moderation.
Harvey: I was referring to your interest, not your capacity.
Emma: So was I.

The Town of No Return provided an immediate benchmark for Season 4, demonstrating how the new, filmed *Avengers* could offer a 'constant interplay' between the traditional television category of 'light entertainment' and a darker, more disturbing drama; between the real and the surreal or bizarre. The Season 4 *Avengers* episodes, at their best, became borderline, 'disruptive' texts which defy labelling, pushing beyond genre.

By contrast, *Dial A Deadly Number* is often seen as an old-fashioned episode, with a heavily-researched script and a video-tape era feel to it. Certainly it has a claustrophobic studio-bound atmosphere; even the car park motorbike scene was filmed inside. However, *Dial A Deadly Number* is also a radically innovative episode which uses verbal and visual wit to disrupt the viewer's sense of watching comfortable, formulaic TV drama.

The 'teaser' sets the tone, introducing a number of key themes. We are immediately given a contrast between tradition/modernity. The 'establishment' is represented by the City bar and company executives; the transistor bleeper is a "new gadget" in Norman Tod-Hunter's words, a symbol of the brave new world of technology.

However, this simplistic polarity will soon become blurred. It is, after all, the traditional, "conservative" Henry Boardman who has introduced the bleepers to his 174 year old bank and his business clients/friends. The new and the old can co-exist as well as collide in this *Avengerland*.

Tod-Hunter's pompous speech – and his life – is ended just as he announces that:

"For our company the outlook is healthy. Very..."

The humour is black and subversive, appearing to poke fun at the smug, exclusive world of banking and finance.

Once again, nothing is as it seems. Steed appears to take great pleasure from the old-world, "archaic" Boardman bank – "the air of ordered calm, a feeling of solidarity" – yet, as we later discover, the bank hierarchy is split. Boardman is a man of scruples and integrity, while John Harvey and Boardman's wife are money-grabbing, corrupt and murderous. Beneath the gentlemen's club feel of Boardman's Bank lie people who will chat to you amiably at a drinks' party but send helmeted hit-men to liquidate you moments later. As Steed remarks to Mrs. Peel after the bikers have tried to kill him:

"A far cry from sherry and biscuits."

This is a world of polished veneer, with danger lurking beneath; where a bleeper can be a harmless answering service or hide a deadly capillary needle.

The witty, verbal exchanges between Steed and Mrs. Peel can, paradoxically, both strengthen and weaken the realism of the plot. When the pair are 'introduced' to each other at the Boardman's penthouse flat, Steed's testing of Emma about her Barbados roots works both as playful jesting and challenging inquisition, almost as if he wants her cover to be blown.

Emma Peel is unflappable and positively thrives in this masculine world, demonstrating her ability to joust verbally with men, defeating them intellectually. This is demonstrated in her exchanges with John Harvey.

Harvey: Do you like wine, Mrs. Peel?
Emma: In moderation.

Harvey: I was referring to your interest, not your capacity.
Emma: So was I.

The wit is polished and Wildean, but has a deeper meaning: Emma Peel is a revolutionary, emancipated female protagonist, unlike any other in the mid-1960s world of British television drama. Being *The Avengers*, though, there is always a less 'straight' side to this gender emancipation. Her confession to Steed that she is studying applied medicine works on two levels. It reflects her intellectual powers – which Steed often defers to – but is also part of a 'running gag' in the season as almost every week she demonstrates yet another area of cerebral (or physical) expertise. In other words, she is 'too good to be true'. *The Avengers* reveals itself as willing to engage with or reflect changing sexual politics but unwilling to be didactic or take itself (too) seriously.

The humour in *Dial A Deadly Number* is often subversive in its ability to cut across the darker, more serious layers of the plot. When Mrs. Peel encounters Fitch for the first time, at the undertaker's, her important search for Tod-Hunter's effects is interrupted by a Goon-like funeral director:

"Tod-Hunter? In mahagony and walnut...velvet lined. Solid brass handles, Gothic style. I prefer the Corinthian fluted myself. Tasteful...Tod-Hunter...yes, he's with us."

The moment breaks the dramatic tension. It is humorous, bizarre, yet strangely naturalistic. After all, to the funeral director, his (dead) clients are simply defined by the boxes they will be buried in.

Fitch's horrific, Hitchcock-like storeroom with its stopped clocks – monuments of the moment of their "release from time" – represents the disturbing underbelly of *The Avengers*. Even here, humour is used to relieve or undermine the tension. As Steed frees the tied-up Mrs. Peel, he announces:

"Barbados/London...cupboard class."

The cleverly-structured script revels in its artificiality with a series of parallel or paired scenes: two butlers presenting sherry and biscuits in the City; two wine-tasting challenges in which first Steed, then Emma, cheat while amazing their opponent; two cellar scenes in the bank vaults: one a spoof duel, one a real battle; two flirting scenes in which Steed is trying to unravel the plot threads; two watch-bomb scenes in which Steed terrifies first Ruth Boardman and then Fitch by pretending to open the casing.

This playful, teasing structure allows scenes to either pre-figure or echo each other, reminding us that there are connections to be made by both the Avengers and the viewers.

The final fight scene in the bank cellar – one of the most famous in the series – provides an iconic *Avengers* moment: the diabolical mastermind knocked out by a champagne cork. This single moment illustrates *The Avengers*' ability to defy genre and constantly surprise its television audience: a storyline which includes one of the most disturbing of characters – the sadistic Fitch and his "orgy of death" – but where villains can be dealt with stylishly. It is a dramatic piece where the influences of Hitchcock, Wilde and *The Goon Show* can all be found within a single episode. *Dial A Deadly Number* draws inspiration from other literary/cultural sources yet provides a highly original, unsettling filmic experience.

DEATH AT BARGAIN PRICES

Horatio Kane: A man can possess a Michelangelo can't he, Steed, and still appreciate a Picasso?

Death at Bargain Prices shares common ground with its immediate predecessor in the production order of the season, *Dial a Deadly Number*. Just as the latter offers a cultural clash between the 'timeless' tradition of London banks such as Boardmans and the modern world of (deadly) gadgets, *Death at Bargain Prices* offers us a surreal setting in which Pinters – a seemingly traditional department store – hides an atomic bomb. However, while this is an episode which draws on many of the show's principal formulaic leitmotifs, it also engages with gender politics in a revolutionary manner.

The 'teaser' is pure *Avengers*. One of Steed's "best agents" is seen searching for something at nighttime in a closed Pinters. An atmospheric sense of menace is created by the sounds of clock chimes, footsteps, the whining of the lift and the creepy-looking toys on display. At the same time this is playfully undercut by the agent's use of the noisy lift which makes any attempt at stealthy espionage impossible. The sound of a silencer shooting him six times – positively "ostentatious" in the words of Mrs. Peel – and the swaying of an inflatable toy become both disturbing and faintly ridiculous simultaneously, leaving the viewer unsettled and unsure whether to take the teaser seriously or not.

The deliberate artificiality or fictionality of the teaser is both reinforced and heightened later on when Horatio Kane's henchmen meet in the camping department in the midst of a display with a forest or jungle theme. It is a set-within-a-set. "House dick" Jarvis is found dead there moments later by Mrs. Peel, his body theatrically displayed with a spear sticking out. 'Ostentatious', once again but, more interestingly, the scene is both self-referential and playful. In *Death at Bargain Prices* Brian Clemens recreates *The Avengers* as a series happy to poke fun at itself and offering a post-modern sense of metafiction.

For much of this episode Mrs. Peel suggests that she and Steed exist on either side of a traditional/modern polarity. If Horatio Kane senses that he belongs in a previous era – "a glorious age, gracious, leisurely, ordered" – Emma feels that Steed is of the same vintage, a remnant of a vanished age:

"The department of discontinued lines. You should fit in rather well."

Steed spends much of his time flirting with women in this episode; both desperately and unsuccessfully, in the case of his attempts to interest Emma Peel. After he is attacked at Pinters, he expects sympathy from his "ministering angel", and then warns her that he is "red-blooded". Emma turns his sexual advances down and is equally unimpressed when Steed tells her how excited he was to be informed that she was now working "in ladies underwear." There is an almost mother/son oedipal battle taking place and Steed's 'charm' is seen as tiring in a storyline where Emma views their quest as an unwelcome diversion from her scientific research. (There is more than a hint of irony about this as a kidnapped, brilliant scientist creating an atomic bomb is at the heart of the matter).

In contrast to Steed's idle, adolescent flirting, Mrs. Peel is busy studying advanced science. Her exploded molecular construction is incomprehensible to Steed who is left to treat it like a child's toy. The paper she is preparing on thermodynamics places her firmly in a technological, modern world, as does her trendy 1960s "Cyclops" eye door. Steed, by contrast, is at ease with his "merry quips" and playful chat-up lines. He seems to be an Edwardian Oscar Wilde figure, in contrast to Peel's hip, modern character.

The sense of two worlds clashing is highlighted by Emma's 'promotion' from sexist lingerie to futuristic space age toys. When the final fight scenes roll, the Steed/Peel dichotomy is still in place. Steed uses a toy gun, then a cricket bat while Emma relies on her fighting abilities to defeat Massey, before using a real gun to kill one of Kane's other henchmen.

There is more than a hint of irony that Mrs. Peel is, according to Farthingale, "dismissed for philandering with the (male) customers" when it is men like John Steed and Pinters' employee Tony Marco who are the sexual predators, always keen to make it clear that they are "open to suggestions".

If Horatio Kane's plan – to "overtake" the country – is formulaic *Avengers*, the threat of an atomic bomb is one which places the episode firmly in a post-war era of Cold War politics and fear. Kane revels in his new-found ability to destroy London with a simple "demonstration of power":

"This store and fifty miles surrounding it will disappear completely from the map."

Farthingale's description of the bomb as "terribly simple" succinctly sums up the horror which this nuclear-threatened, push-button age offers. It is a vision of mass-destruction at the touch of a switch.

Despite this central storyline, the main thematic concern in *Death at Bargain Prices* is the modern war between the sexes, rather than a nuclear one. The episode belongs to a countercultural mid-1960s era in which some women – epitomized here by Emma Peel – were seizing control of their own lives, moving with the times or even, perhaps, forcing the times to move with them.

Men are given two choices: accept that traditional male/female roles are changing, boundaries blurring, or if not then, like John Steed, they may become objects in Kane's hived-off, museum-like department of discontinued lines. There is something faintly ridiculous and old-fashioned about the department store itself. Steed is quick to poke fun at the use of a formal, hierarchical language in Pinters: "Our Mr. Massey…Our Mrs. Peel…" etc. It is almost as if its stuffy, class-defining world does, indeed, need blowing up.

By the end of this episode Steed and Peel are seen happily working in tandem to prevent the bomb being detonated. They ride off on Pinters bikes together, heading towards that bright, happy horizon. Nevertheless, awkward questions have been posed which remain with the viewer after the formulaic ending has (seemingly) brought things to a neat point of closure.

Death at Bargain Prices centres on a heated war of gender rather than a Cold War of nuclear weapons and espionage. It is for this reason that this claustrophobic, studio-based episode has a key role to play in a groundbreaking season for *The Avengers*.

TOO MANY CHRISTMAS TREES

Steed: What made you invite me down here in the first place?
Emma: The thought just entered my head.

Reading Tony Williamson's draft script for *Too Many Christmas Trees* reveals a fairly straightforward plot. A man with telepathic powers discovers that by combining with others their grouping increases the power through 'mental rapport'. Picking out victims who guard top-secret information – including Steed – they use projected images to send terrifying dreams into the sleepers, breaking down their mental defence systems. When a victim is completely broken, questions can be 'fed' and secrets then subconsciously leak out.

I produce this short plot summary to highlight the fact that little else of the story makes its way into the final filmed version. The original script – dream sequences aside – was an intriguingly far-fetched idea but the treatment was fairly sober and humourless. This was obviously also the opinion of the production team as they then set about 'avengerising' it. (If the word didn't exist, it does now!) While Brian Clemens' reworking of scripts did not always have a positive effect, what finally emerges in *Too Many Christmas Trees* is a quite remarkable, surreal delight, one of the high points of the season.

Given *The Avengers*' interest in blurring the boundaries between realism/surrealism, it is unsurprising that dream sequences make their way into a number of episodes, including *Silent Dust* and, more significantly, Season 5's *Death's Door*.

In *Too Many Christmas Trees* the 'teaser' takes us into Steed's nightmarish dream which has been provided for him by the diabolical mastermind. The images are wonderfully surreal and artificial: polystyrene balls of snow cover the ground; Steed walks through a forest of ten foot *Magic Roundabout*-style trees before encountering a treasure-trove of enormous presents and a masked Father Christmas.

At one point Steed sees a pair of festive stockings (filled with gifts) which transforms before his/our eyes into a stockinged corpse. The artificiality *enhances* the disturbing, dramatic effect rather than minimizing it. We are compelled to share Steed's fear, despite the DIY crudeness of the dream. The mysterious high vibrations of the 'dream music' play a similar role in the story to the whine of the milk float in *The Hour that Never Was*, co-creating the creepy atmosphere alongside the images.

Whereas in *Silent Dust* Steed's cowboy dream is simply an amusing diversion, here the oneiric narrative sequences play a central role. Rather than setting up a reality/dream polarity, *Too Many Christmas Trees* offers us a far more complex, fused vision. The dreams are real – in the sense of creations injected from a real world – while many of the 'real' things Steed will encounter and experience in Brandon Storey's house are fantasies.

Storey is obsessed by Charles Dickens and fills his mansion with Dickensian paraphernalia. Steed encounters many of the 'real' objects seen in his dream in this 'fabricated' house. In contrast, items seen first in reality – such as the guillotine cigar cutter – then reappear in projected nightmares, as when Steed is beheaded by the laughing Father Christmas (while Madame Guillotine places the wicker bread basket in front of him).

There is a playfully self-referential touch early on in the episode when Steed opens a Christmas card from Mrs. Gale and – in an indirect reference to Honor Blackman's role as Pussy Galore in the Bond film *Goldfinger* – wonders:

"Whatever can she be doing in Fort Knox?"

However, it is Storey's house that is at the heart of the episode's intertextual richness. The fancy dress party requires the guests to dress as Dickens characters. This allows for a memorable scene which illustrates *The Avengers*' ability to merge dramatic, dark strands with a metafictional surrealism. Mrs. Peel (Oliver Twist) is due to meet reluctant villain Jeremy Wade (Marley's Ghost) in The Hall of Great Expectations which Storey has converted into a set: Miss Haversham's wedding feast. Despite the layers of fictionality this scenario requires us to take on board, the atmospheric scene is played 'straight', with Mrs. Peel's shock at discovering Wade's cobwebbed corpse genuine and touching.

We are caught up in the drama *despite* ourselves. After all, the scene involves already fictional characters dressed as characters from two Dickens' texts meeting on the set of a third one, which in turn is, of course, an *Avengers* set. This playful set-within-the-set is a recurring, self-referential device of Season 4.

Too Many Christmas Trees cheats its audience in a number of ways, playing mind games with us, just as the mastermind does with Steed and Mrs. Peel. Dr. Teasel is precisely that, a tease (just as Storey re-tells Dickens). If we aren't taken in by Teasel's sinister appearance and cynicism at the party – the owner tells Steed/us that he has never met the man before – then we certainly fall for the cheat when he holds Mrs. Peel at gunpoint.

We are then tricked (with Mrs. Peel) into thinking that Steed has been drugged. Extending our willing suspension of disbelief to snapping point, we are asked to accept – against all the earlier evidence – that it is Mrs. Peel who is being 'interfered with' (mentally speaking, that is). It isn't just the diabolical mastermind playing mind games, then. Steed, Teasel and the story itself combine to make us question everything we see and are told. We are never quite sure if Steed is playing with us/the masterminds or not:

Wade: I trust you found your way down here all right.
Steed: Instinctively.

The playfulness reaches a crescendo in the final sequences of *Too Many Christmas Trees*. Searching for their enemy, Steed and Mrs. Peel simultaneously spy a naked female bust – out of place amidst the Dickensia – and twist it to reveal a secret passage. Despite the pressing need to act quickly, chivalrous Steed stops himself from using the protruding buttocks to turn the mechanism.

The fight scene – in a room of distorting mirrors – sees Mrs. Peel pause to rearrange her Oliver Twist outfit. The illusions multiply as the director films the actors' faces and fighting sequences through the mirrors themselves, lending both a confusing dramatic layer – has Steed really been shot? – while also providing a comedic surrealism to an already bizarre fight with Father Christmas. On a symbolic level, the distorting mirrors reflect what *The Avengers* was offering in terms of television drama.

The visual effects and Roy Baker's direction are experimental and atmospheric. The aerial views of the telepathists' mind-map table are highly effective, as are the superimposed images of Janice Crane and Steed during her mental inquisition of him. We see Mrs. Peel's reaction to the cobwebbed corpse from the corpse's viewpoint, through the cobwebs themselves. Finally, that wonderful mirror scene is a visual highlight of the entire series, offering at the same time homage to Dickens' fascination with mirrors.

This book centres on the themes, plots, characters, images and leitmotifs etc., rather than the acting. However, it should be mentioned here how central to *The Avengers*' artistic and commercial success was the on-screen rapport of Macnee and Rigg. While this is partly down to the wonderfully-written dialogue, it also has a lot to do with their fine acting as individuals and as a 'couple'.

Too Many Christmas Trees brings the characters closer together than ever before, as would the remarkable first half of *The Hour that Never Was*. Steed, in a rare moment of heartfelt frankness, admits to Mrs. Peel that:

"You're the only person I confide in."

It is generally accepted that the actors had a similarly close working relationship. They played a key role in the innovative quirkiness of Season 4, often adding their own ideas or improvisations. Their ability to play the comic and dramatic elements equally well is never more apparent than in *Too Many Christmas Tree*, nor is their skill at re-creating the rapport of the central characters. When Steed appraises Mrs. Peel as Oliver Twist it is clear that his remark – "my word you *have* filled out" – amuses them both as actors and characters. The chemistry between them is almost tangible.

Too Many Christmas Trees may cheat us – in terms of storyline – but it is a playful, self-referential, witty episode which provides us with subversion and champagne which flow together in a unique, festive package.

As a footnote, Bernard Ginez's exploration of this episode on the French website *Le Monde des Avengers*, drew my attention to the 1945 horror film, *Dead of Night*, which Mervyn Johns (Storey) had starred in twenty years before. In *Dead of Night*, Johns plays an architect who arrives at a country house for a party only to reveal to everyone that he has seen them all before, in a dream. The experimental film is structured through a number of 'sequences', one directed by avenger Charles Crichton, and includes Christmas party and Haunted Mirror sections. Could this film have been a major influence on the episode and does this explain the casting of the actor? There is certainly a subversive, surreal horror at play in *Too Many Christmas Trees* which playfully collides with the sparkling wit, charm and mistletoe; Johns' presence adds another intertextual layer to this rich *Avengers* hour.

Charles Dickens is the perfect writer to be connected to *The Avengers*: in both Dickens' fiction and the series' best episodes we have a fascinating interplay between realism and surrealism, macabre drama and melodrama, as traditional genre boundaries are revolutionarily blurred.

THE CYBERNAUTS

Steed: People aren't machines. Of *course*, they're fallible. *That's* what makes them human!

On a simplistic level, *The Cybernauts* is classic *Avengers*, providing the show with both one of its most well-known, instantly recognizable iconic images – the humanized metallic robot – and one of its most recognizable sounds, the "sharp, whip-like" noise of its lethal karate chop. However, despite its continuing popularity among *Avengers* fans, it remains one of the season's misunderstood gems. Often reduced by viewers' memories to this single image, the episode has a complex, subtle plot. Beneath the sci-fi glamour of the robots themselves lies a fascinating philosophical/political debate about a technological revolution, the new computerised age which was emerging in the 1960s.

Modern technology is often at the heart of the diabolical masterminds' plans in *The Avengers*, as much a part of its formulaic approach as the series of connected murders which usually takes place. This has led some critics to consider the show to be conservative or even Luddite in its attitude to cultural change. While there may be an element of truth to this, *The Cybernauts* engages with the 'new age' debate in an interesting, non-simplistic way.

Once again we are offered a contrast between Emma Peel's modernity – the leather outfit, trendy circular steel fireplace, contemporary sports car – and John Steed with his traditional umbrella, bowler hat and vintage car. In Philip Levene's original script Peel comes round to Steed's way of thinking at the end of their cybernaut experience. Just as Steed is looking forward to escaping the "hustle and bustle" of the modern city for the "primitive countryside", Peel shares Steed's sense of nostalgia:

"You know, Steed, there are times when I wish somehow we could turn the clock back."

This idea was scrapped in the final version, presumably because it rings false with Peel's cool, ultra-modern image. However, unlike in *Death at Bargain Prices*, the main clash of ideas or ideals in *The Cybernauts* sees Steed in conflict with one of the most interesting and subtle masterminds of the series, Dr. Armstrong.

This sense of opposition is embedded in the opening scenes through the musical scores, the cybernaut attacks carrying an "eerie, menacing theme" while Steed's arrival at the first crime scene is accompanied by "ironical, lilting" music. This simplistic divide is undermined as the plot unfolds.

As Steed acknowledges, Armstrong is not driven by greed or money. We are told that he was kicked out of the Ministry because he "refused to toe the official line". Ministry employee Gilbert tells Steed:

"Felt we should be 'constructive' rather than destructive. Had some crazy idea for building some machine for clearing debris in radio-active areas".

Gilbert's patronizing dismissal of Armstrong's vision offers us a critique of government policy, the Ministry of Defence as a Ministry of *Offence*, run by administrators who are unwilling to explore peace-driven ideas. Steed's agreement with Gilbert seems to place him on the 'wrong' side of a war/peace philosophy.

Armstrong is an intriguing, developed character even before we meet him. Steed is made to wait until he encounters him, increasing the sense of mystery. When he does eventually visit United Automation, under the guise of a journalist, we experience the first part of their philosophical/political debate about modern technology, continued when Steed is taken prisoner later on.

Armstrong shares Japanese businessman Tusamo's excitement at the sense of a new technological revolution, "the age of push-button" as he calls it. Unlike Tusamo, Armstrong is not financially-driven. He offers Steed a series of inter-connected polarities:

humans/machines; temperamental/obedient; unreliable/trouble-free.

His plan of an army of cybernauts is fuelled by a desire for error-proof "government by automation", or, as Steed prefers to describe it, "electronic dictatorship". Their ideological debate, shortened in the final cut, is an intriguing one:

Steed: *This* your idea of progress?
Armstrong: If I can prevent the ultimate catastrophe.
Steed: But at what price? A Cybernetic police state. People aren't machines. Of *course*, they're fallible. *That's* what makes them human!

Armstrong's bright vision of a machine-led Utopia is, for Steed, a nightmarish Dystopia in which choice, free-thinking, and liberty will have been suppressed. The argument is a cleverly-constructed one with Armstrong eloquently illustrating how easily human error could lead to nuclear war. Steed's stance is that this constant menace or risk is a price worth paying to enjoy the human (imperfect) world which has invented pleasures such as classical music and Martinis. Partly due to Armstrong's social conscience we are forced to question whether the simplistic goodie/baddie binarism can be comfortably maintained here.

The cybernaut figures themselves carry a sense of irony. In order to make the world safe, Armstrong will dehumanize it. Yet at the heart of his robotic creation is a humanizing process: the first cybernaut doesn't simply look human – which it has to in its role as serial killer

– it has been given a name (Roger) and its inventor describes it as his "child". Roger may have been invented as a "guided missile" but Armstrong feels the (all-too human) need to humanize him. Even Roger's weapon has been taken from the ancient art of karate rather than new-fangled technology.

In an episode with so many red herrings – we suspect Tusamo, Sensai and Jephcott before we even see Armstrong – there is a sense that nothing is as simple as it first seems. John Steed is forced out of his (complacent) comfort zone in *The Cybernauts*. His casual, playful approach – illustrated by the way he brushes his umbrella across the grooved interior of Armstrong's circular lift – is replaced by a genuine sense of fear on his second visit to the factory. The concern is not solely for Mrs. Peel's safety but for that of the human race itself. This fear, ironically, is based on the potential *end* to the Cold War and the nuclear threat which Armstrong's success may enable. We don't actually see a cybernaut clearly until half an hour of the episode has been played out, adding further irony to the fact that this philosophical episode tends to be remembered for the single image of a robotic figure, rather than the thoughtful, intriguing debate which it revolves around.

Steed: Will the machine supplant Man? Or woman, for that matter?
Emma: And will it?

'Undercover' Steed is preparing for his forthcoming interview with Armstrong and his tone – at this early stage in the story – is characteristically light-hearted. With the benefit of hindsight, the scene is actually darkly ironic. Emma Peel's question does not receive a straightforward 'yes' or 'no' answer from him, in an episode which defies our television viewer's desire for closure.

THE

GRAVEDIGGERS

Sir Horace Winslip: What is going on?...What extraordinary people.

"Welcome to Winslip Junction, Sir. Where all the lines converge, and all friends meet."

Sir Horace Winslip's greeting to Steed when he arrives at the eccentric home of the railway magnet sums up the way in which *The Gravediggers* manages to bring together so many of the themes, images and leitmotifs of *The Avengers*: the Cold War, nuclear power, the dangers of modern technology, cemeteries, funerals, steam trains, wildly eccentric characters all 'converge' in an episode which offers the viewer a delightfully strange mixture of visual and verbal ingredients. Funerals booked months in advance, coffins with holes to breathe through, hearses delivering *to* hospitals, surgeons using blowtorches and micrometers, nurses carrying pistols. It is no surprise that Steed drily admires "the tireless activity of the staff" at the Sir Horace Winslip Hospital for Ailing Railwaymen.

The 'teaser' offers us an image used so often in *The Avengers*, that of a burial. However, the light-hearted funereal music score acts as a form of delayed decoding, warning us that the death is staged. If the invisible nuclear threat is a concern in both *Death at Bargain Prices* and *The Cybernauts*, then it is at the heart of this episode. Introduced immediately after the 'teaser', the deadly plot to use a number of newly-invented jamming devices to black out the radar screens at early warning stations appears to be a completely realistic scenario:

"A missile attack could be launched on this country without any warning whatsoever until it was too late."

Marlow, like Dr. Armstrong, has left the Ministry, frustrated by a lack of government funding. His faked death and the use of cemeteries as points on the map to create a jammed radar zone are accepted by a television audience in terms of realism. However, in true *Avengers* fashion this is then undermined by a number of bizarre scenes. Johnson and his hospital theatre staff 'operate' on (*aka* assemble) machines using regulation medical rubber gloves, masks etc. He orders the nurse to pass him "forceps... scalpel...blowtorch..." From real to surreal, the plot seamlessly moves between the two with consummate ease.

If the Hospital for Ailing Railwaymen is a front then Winslip Junction is a flamboyant example of *Avengerland*, its owner a wonderfully eccentric man from a vanished age of steam. The fact that he is unwittingly the financial provider for the diabolical mastermind is another example of the way the 'lines converge' in this episode. As for Winslip Junction itself, Sir Horace's house and grounds have been converted into a railway fantasy: the doorbell is a train whistle, the hall a booking office, entrance is by platform ticket rather than formal invitation.

As was the case in *Death at Bargain Prices* with the camping department, here the interior train carriage and station form a set-within-a-set, offering the viewers two layers of artificiality. John Steed's comment that the station set is "remarkable" is that of an actor/character, creating a clever level of self-referentiality. Steed, after all, is expected to play his role in the fantasy in return for a first-class lunch on board.

If the house itself represents a stage-on-a-stage then the miniature railway line is a 'real' toy train set arranged on an outside location. Sir Horace's folly becomes that of the writer and director as the final scenes take the plot to a new level of eccentric playfulness.

"The iron horse, magnificent creature...and all being murdered by the motor car."

With Emma Peel tied to the train track, there is the (unlikely) possibility that Winslip's tirade about the death of the railways will be turned on its head. Here it is the train which could prove to be murderous, a miniature one at that. Any sense of a serious climax is undermined, first by the musical score which recreates the atmosphere of a second-rate 1920s silent movie, with Mrs. Peel playing the damsel in distress. Even Johnson's henchmen, so menacing earlier on in the hospital, have joined in the fun, seen grinning as they stoke the engine and prepare to mow her down. Steed waits on the platform, bending his knees, newspaper in hand, 'playing' the role of a waiting commuter. The subsequent fights onboard the tiny train become those of little boys playing. Sir Horace – who is initially portrayed as a likeable, if gullible, eccentric - has a second, darker layer. He is happy to fund the destruction of the British car industry for egotistical reasons – rather than green politics – and when he spies Mrs. Peel tied to the tracks he is solely concerned that his train may be damaged:

"What is going on? What is that young woman doing tied to the railway line...she'll break the engine."

He is a caricature of a spoilt little boy who has never grown up. The last-ditch rescue of Mrs. Peel is simply part of the silent movie/*Avengers* formula, lacking any dramatic tension. Having already played the role of a nurse – "you are not here to think, but to obey" – she has simply taken on another thankless acting role, one which connects her to female 'victims' in previous eras of film-making.

The tag scene, in which Steed and Peel enjoy a train ride, reversing down the tracks from the scene of her potential death towards a 'bright horizon' is symbolic of an episode where everything is both more and less than it seems, where nothing functions as it would do in a rational world.

In *Avengerland* 'toy' trains can be deadly, coffins are taken into operating theatres, florists sell radar jamming parts and grand country houses are converted into elaborate sets where rich old men can play out their fantasies.

The fact that these 'harmless' fantasies are intrinsically connected to the deadly plans to sabotage the country's defence system is the perfect example of how in *The Gravediggers* all lines do indeed converge, even those which traditionally separate realism from surrealism and formulaic genre from innovative television drama. The episode epitomizes the subversive champagne of the season, providing viewers with both froth and substance.

ROOM WITHOUT A VIEW

Chessman: A unique service. Information, at leisure.

Room Without A View begins with close-ups of a series of fat, grinning, porcelain figures which become more and more bizarre, the final ones surrounded by baby gargoyles. The music matches the Oriental theme, the wind-chimes adding to the general atmosphere of an exotic 'otherness'. The swaying curtains become theatrical as they are gripped by a hand which then shakes as it rips a photo, before attempting to strangle the real-life woman whose still-life image we have just seen torn up. Once again, the teaser has offered us an unsettling mix of the 'real' and the surreal.

The post-teaser scene simultaneously reinforces and undermines social stereotypes. Vernals – from the Ministry – is the civil servant geek, an "eager beaver, everything in triplicate", governed by the theoretical rulebook of "standard procedure" yet totally useless when the threat becomes physically real. He patronisingly assumes that a woman will be lost in the male-dominated worlds of science and psychology. Rather than being bamboozled by the technical jargon, Mrs. Peel simply demystifies the language. 'Cryogenics' is translated as "the science of cooling things"; specialist, esoteric expressions such as "intensified re-orientation and auto-suggestion" become simplified to "brainwashed". Vernals criticises Steed for his (perceived) lack of textbook knowledge about the Nee San prison, only to be shocked – as we perhaps are – by Steed's in-depth analysis:

"Rice husks, gruel, shavings of bad pork and water. *Brackish* water tasting of dust. Some friendly sort of place, Nee San. You have nothing to do all day but lie in a cell listening to the world go by...marching feet, fog-horns on the ships going up river, and the chiming of the clock. And there's no sense of time because whatever the hour in Nee San, the clock always strikes three."

Steed is not just a suave salesman of adventures; he is also a great raconteur, able to paint a picture with words, offering us a pre-echo of the Nee San set we will see later. His description has Mrs. Peel, Vernals and us spellbound. Steed is always capable of surprise. Racial stereotypes are playfully dealt with, Chinese Anna Wadkin telling Steed that "inscrutability" is meant to be her quality, not his.

Emma Peel's humane qualities are revealed as Vernals and Dr. Cullen dismiss John Wadkin as a "cabbage" and "a fish in a tank" respectively, while she perseveres, attempting to communicate with this wrecked man.

Vernals is a ridiculous figure, as his over-the-top spying techniques at the Chessman Hotel remind us. Steed's facial expression, as they silently communicate in the lobby, acknowledges this. The Chessman offers us sets within the set, chessboards springing up everywhere: reception, lobby, lift, and corridor. Even the doors of the lift are decorated in chess graphics and the bedside lampshade bases are knights. When hotel manager Carter proudly explains the playful set-up, he could almost be talking about *The Avengers* itself:

"For your amusement...you may pit your wits against the grand master. The games are changed every day."

However, the chessboards – like the show's formula – provide a sense of continuity. The mystery of how Cullen and seven other physicists have "disappeared into thin air" is, like a game of chess, a puzzle which Steed is left to solve. As Steed searches Cullen's vacated room, he even pauses to move a chess piece, playfully reinforcing the chess game leitmotif in *Room Without A View*:

Steed: Fascinating game, chess. Pitting of wits, strategy, point, counter-point. Not unlike war.

As Steed and Vernals reflect on their failure to prevent another leading scientist from vanishing, we get a typically witty Steedism:

Vernals: Um...who's going to tell the Minister?
Steed: I will. Probably have to hand in my umbrella.

The humour in this leisurely-paced episode continues as Mrs. Peel attempts to refuse to go undercover again: "I've had my fill of *fascinating new experiences.*" The comment mimics Steed's, and reflects his often underhand use of Emma Peel in dangerous undercover roles, as well as offering us a self-referential touch. If Rigg plays a role each week, so too does Emma. Steed's take up of a role himself, that of Monsieur Gourmet, will allow light-hearted humour to interplay with a dramatic undercurrent in the second half of this episode.

The disturbing drama re-establishes itself as Pasold investigates Cullen's room. The moment he pulls back the curtains to reveal a metal board, rather than the spectacular cityscape view, we have been set a puzzle. How is room 621 transformed from luxurious en-suite accommodation to claustrophobic gas chamber? From the hotel bedroom trap we are taken straight in to another one, the Nee San prison. The sounds which greet Cullen/us echo Steed's earlier description of Nee San, yet the presence of Cullen and the chess piece he is gripping warn us not to be taken in by this set-within-the-set. Wadkin's voice through the vent asks us to question where we are and even whether we really are still in 1965. The prison cell, with its basic walls and straw-strewn floor is simple yet atmospheric. One can easily imagine losing track of time here, of slowly losing one's mind even.

When we finally encounter the mastermind, Max Chessman, his round face bears a dramatic, striking resemblance to the grinning porcelain figures of the teaser. His masochistic secondhand savouring of the gourmet food is oddly humorous and warns us to expect a future scene in which he will encounter Monsieur Gourmet himself. Like a chess grand master, we should be anticipating the future moves. When Mrs. Peel, now reluctantly installed as receptionist, discovers that Steed will be "gourmandising" with Chessman while she works, she warns him with a hint of bitterness: "Well, don't come to me for the bicarbonate of soda."

Max Chessman is a diabolical mastermind with a plan to take his hotel empire further than Napoleon, east of the Black Sea. However, he is also a physical oddity:

"Look at me, one of nature's jokes, a fat man with thin blood. I have to keep the temperature at a steady eighty degrees."

Steed's ridiculously remarkable vineyard knowledge in *Dial A Deadly Number* is matched here as he offers his expert opinion of the proffered cigar: "Cuban, sun-dried, hand-rolled, rolled against the thigh of *une jeune fille*." His description is humorous, but is also a cunningly playful one, as he is stalling while Chessman impatiently awaits the answer to an earlier question about Wadkin. The crispness of the verbal exchanges as Chessman tests Steed's cuisine knowledge is matched by the suspicious Carter grilling Mrs. Peel, the scenes mirroring each other:

Carter: For a receptionist you undertake a great many tasks, Mrs. Peel.
Emma: As a receptionist, Mr. Carter, I expect to.

Her discovery of Pasold's corpse in a laundry basket – the lid popping up conveniently to enable us/her to see inside – offers us a surreal coffin and enables the viewer to place the three sets/puzzle pieces together: hotel, laundry and prison are all housed under the same roof, intertwined enterprises/narratives. There is also a cyclical feeling developing, as Mrs. Peel is trapped – like Pasold before her – in Room 621. Her experience offers us an uncomfortable sense of *déjà vu*. This time, though, the scene takes us further, as a guard in gas mask emerges from the built-in wardrobe. However, if we appear to be making progress then the arrival of Steed in 621 moments later sets us back: the view is back and there is no hint of either gas or foul play. We may be a step ahead of Steed but we are caught in a puzzle maze.

As *Room Without A View* reaches its climax, there is still time for leisured humour as Russian minister Pushkin complains about the nineteen seconds it took for the lift to arrive: "This would not be tolerated at home." Just as the Chessman is in the traditional service industry for its 'normal' guests, a more clandestine one is offered, as Chessman explains:

"A unique service. Information, at leisure, without risk...ready for questioning under ideal conditions."

Chessman's master plan is that of a businessman. He wants to create a global gourmet empire, an upmarket chain in which Chessman becomes a worldwide brand. This makes him very different from most other *Avengers* diabolical masterminds. His physical weakness also makes him strangely vulnerable, pathetically pleading as Steed lowers the room temperature. Once again, Steed finds time to move a chess piece as he waits for Chessman to reveal the whereabouts of Mrs. Peel. This seems appropriate as Steed's unravelling of the strange case is like that of a chess grand master.

With only five minutes remaining, Chessman finally explains the mystery behind room 621: there is a fake version on the seventh floor. Steed's arrival in the room adds a third circle to the cycle, yet the atmosphere this time reassures us that he will not be trapped. As Steed discovers the hidden door in the back of the wardrobe, he still has time to replace the coat hanger, a typical Steed gesture which offers further evidence that all will be well now while reinforcing our image of him as being almost meticulously camp.

Everything appears to be false in *Room Without A View*: the hotel manager, the seventh floor room, the Far East prison and its 'everyday' noises. Even some of the guards and laundry men are no more Chinese than Steed is. It is appropriate, then, that both Steed and Mrs. Peel are also fakes – galloping gourmet and roving receptionist – actors playing roles on the hotel set. The fight finale is played out in front of the tape recorder, Steed employing a mop against the guards' bayonets. The tape reverses just as the villains' fortunes do – matching a similar scenario in *The Master Minds* – and the scene revels in its quirky artificiality, as does the tag scene in which a speeded-up Steed takes Mrs. Peel off in a runaway rickshaw, along a familiar stretch of deserted country road, towards that bright horizon.

Despite the very strong supporting cast – which includes Peter Jeffrey, Philip Latham and Peter Arne – this is one of those rare unloved Season 4 episodes. Roger Marshall's script is well structured, the initial idea is a clever one, yet, despite the presence of wit and humour, the episode never quite develops the charm or the claustrophobically avengerish atmosphere which offer that subversive champagne which we discover in other studio-bound episodes such as *Death at Bargain Prices*, *Dial A Deadly Number*, or *The Cybernauts*. It is, perhaps, the lack of any experimental and quirky camera shots, or unusual, memorable scenes that holds *Room Without A View* back from being anything more than simply well-made.

A SURFEIT OF H$_2$O

Martin: He's not wearing a mackintosh.
Sturm: Pity. Looks like rain.

In a season in which *The Avengers* consistently demonstrates its ability to offer an almost bewildering variety of themes and stylistic approaches, in which each episode is lovingly created as an individual 'film', *A Surfeit of H$_2$0* arguably represents the most individualistic of the lot. It is the only script contributed by Colin Finbow and the fact that Steed and Emma Peel leave their usual cars at home, driving around together in the roofless, jeep-like Mini Moke, highlights the one-off nature of this memorably bizarre episode.

The teaser sees a country man setting wire traps in a field against the backdrop of rumbling thunder, representing both pathetic fallacy and a physical result of the experiments undertaken at the neighbouring wine factory. A sudden rainstorm erupts and the man drowns, lying there with his mouth opening and closing like a fish. It is an unsettling sight. In the post-teaser scene all that is left of him is a puddle in the shape of a man. This surreal image will be repeated later in the episode, and adds a hauntingly odd touch, almost like a liquid scene-of-crime tape.

Steed is in playful mode throughout *A Surfeit of H$_2$0*. He describes the drowned man, Ted Barker, in alliteratively poetic terminology, leaving it to Emma Peel to translate into layman's terms:

Steed: Snare setter, pheasant fancier, partridge pincher...
Emma: You mean the local poacher.

While both the Avengers acknowledge the inexplicable occurrence of a man drowning in a field – "impossible" (Emma); "strange" (Steed) – locals such as Eli Barker and Jonah Barnard consider the weather to be an Old Testament-style portent, a "sign". Their names tell us that they are strange, biblical figures, Eli talking to

Mrs. Peel about demons in his leaking cottage and Jonah preaching about a coming flood in his barn where he is constructing an oak-framed Noah's Ark. If both figures are gently mocked by Steed and the script, Barnard's evidence of strange changes is not simply based on religious superstition; it is also founded on 'surreal reality': marshland butterflies and birds appearing in this historically dry area of the country; the scientific disturbance of the natural world:

"The balance of nature is disturbed; doom is in the air...the same cloud in the same position in the sky every day."

The episode is remarkable for its striking images. Steed's face is strangely distorted as he stares into the glass bottle of the preserved giant cucumber; Eli's face disconcertingly odd as he lies dead in the wine factory's water supply, eyes and mouth wide open. Humans – like Mother Nature – are suffering from the unnatural experimentation at Granny Gregson's.

The humour in *A Surfeit of H$_2$O* is as bizarre as the plot. Steed, under cover as a philandering wine merchant, goes wonderfully over-the-top in his sensual eulogy about wine when offered a lifeless catalogue:

"Catalogue! 'Honeyed blackberry wine'. That means nothing to me, Miss Jason. Where is the tang of blue blackberries gathered in the early morning dew by barefoot peasant girls? The rich nectar taste of honey syrup...The sun glinting on amber liquid...The nostrils assaulted by the heady aromatics of a perfect bouquet...Rolling smooth syrup-sweet liquid around the mouth, alerting the taste buds, savouring the sheer sensuality of a unique experience."

The shocked reaction of the receptionist is almost that of a blushing virgin, and the strangely humorous scene is made odder still by the portrait of Granny Gregson holding an enormous (phallic?) cucumber. Steed does a double take as he looks at the painting, encouraging us to do the same thing. There is plenty of cute/corny humour in the script, Mrs. Peel announcing that her knowledge of meteorological science is "bright in patches"; Steed's tasting of "old bark wine" leading to his assessment that they "must have put the dog in it too".

When the aptly-named Dr. Sturm (German for storm) introduces Steed to one of his state-of-the-art pulping presses – describing it as "a gentle giant" – we are pre-warned that the machine will serve a far more ominous function later on. Indeed, as *A Surfeit of H$_2$0* reaches its dramatic climax, the darker drama bubbles to the surface like fermenting alcohol.

The introduction of Sir Arnold Kelly, a renowned meteorological expert, provides us with a typical *Avengers* victim: short-sighted, affably eccentric, and lost in his own world.

Martin: He's not wearing a mackintosh.
Sturm: Pity. Looks like rain.

As Sir Arnold drowns in another torrential downpour – taking us back to the teaser – the disturbing images are heightened by the sight of Sturm watching impassively from the laboratory window. It is a disconcertingly chilling sight. The shape of the surreal puddle is commented on by Steed who states that "I had an aunty who used to make biscuits like this." The bizarre connection Steed makes is as surreal as the image itself.

The climax of the plot dramatically switches between Emma Peel being tortured in the pulping press and Steed and Jonah journeying through the wine factory's drains.

Sturm: Another half an inch before breathing becomes difficult…a fraction more pressure and your ribs will bend, another fraction and your ribs will crack.

Emma Peel's pained facial expressions are genuinely disturbing, the potentially clichéd scene played effectively straight as Sturm promises to "squeeze the information" out of her. The idea that his ability to control rain "to order" represents the "biggest military weapon since the nuclear bomb" does not seem particularly far-fetched and, suddenly, Jonah's warnings about the dangers of scientific experimentation no longer seem ridiculously alarmist:

"Man has destroyed mountains with his science…Making rain! It's flying in the face of nature!"

As in *Man-Eater of Surrey Green* and *Silent Dust*, the potential ecological dangers created by scientists are made to appear very 'real', in the sense of possible. Steed's arrival – just in the nick of time – allows humour to disrupt the drama:

Steed: What are you, the sparkle in the seaweed soda?
Emma: No, I'm the kick in the nettle noggin.

Despite Steed's reassurance that he understands how to operate Sturm's machine, we are left unsure whether Steed has cleverly outwitted the pulp press or simply guessed correctly as he releases Mrs. Peel from the mechanical jaws. As his bowler is crushed, Emma Peel playfully reassures him that "it was over very quickly. I don't think it suffered." Once again, the humour here is surreal, playing on the idea of the faithful bowler almost being a canine companion.

The final fight scene which takes place in driving rain is as bizarre as the scenes which precede it, as two worlds/times collide: Jonah offering his Old Testament refrain of "Hallelujah! The flood is here!" while Sturm is appropriately dealt with, drowning in his own ultra-modern rain machine. The machine offers four choices – drizzle, shower, storm, tempest – and, like the drama itself, has been pushed into the highest 'gear' for this dramatic finale.

The tag scene of *A Surfeit of H$_2$O* does not require a themed-vehicle such as a hearse, rickshaw, milk float, or magic carpet. It already has one in the shape of the Mini Moke, a one-off, quirky mode of transport which zooms off towards that 'bright horizon', a symbol of this oddly-entertaining, unique episode.

(A short interview with Colin Finbow appears in the back of this book, pp. 208-209).

MAN-EATER OF SURREY GREEN

Steed: I'm a herbicidal maniac!

Man-Eater of Surrey Green isn't any more fantastical than the cult science fiction novel *The Day of the Triffids*. The key difference is that Wyndham's novel is able to terrify readers because the images are co-created by our vivid imaginations; we paint the pictures, as it were. With television and cinema we are forced to rely on the images provided for us by the writer and director. These nearly always fall short of those projected by our over-active minds. It is, after all, one of the great advantages of books. Thankfully, this only becomes a problem in the final few minutes of this *Avengers* episode.

The teaser for *Man-Eater of Surrey Green* sees amorous botanists Alan Carter and Laura Burford at work in a ministry greenhouse before plant-loving Burford encounters a strange hypnotic sound which sends her trampling through precious plants and bushes as if she is sleepwalking, before getting into a waiting, chauffeur-driven car. Carter is oblivious to the strange events, his hearing aid encasing (and protecting) him in his own private world of research. The sight of zombified figures – effectively portrayed in *The Master Minds* – will be repeated or re-used throughout this story. However, it is, arguably, the strange sound which creates the unsettling atmosphere, here, rather than the sight of the 'walking dead'.

The post-teaser scene sees Steed playing his formulaic role of suave salesman of adventures, offering a rose to the suspicious Mrs. Peel:

"What nasty situation have you got in store for me this time, hm? You have your own built-in early warning system, you know. A certain look in the eye."

Emma Peel is not simply demonstrating her ability to read Steed's cunning, underhand nature. She is voicing our own ability to recognise the series' formulaic approach as Steed takes her/us off for another extraordinary adventure. For us, the 'early warning system' is the music and opening credits as we (voluntarily) head off for our weekly fix of fantasy.

The experimental direction of Sidney Hayers is one of the highlights of *Man-Eater of Surrey Green*. The quirkiness of the camera work is first in evidence as Steed visits Sir Lyle Peterson's country home. As he stands in the entrance porch, we get a close-up of Steed examining a strange plant, the image framed by its strange 'tentacles'. This odd sight – which offers us a playful piece of delayed decoding – is immediately swapped for another, as Lennox, the powerfully-built young butler, answers the door. Lacking the world-weary charm of most *Avengers* butlers, he is menacingly resplendent in boots and an old-fashioned, buttoned-up tunic; more guard dog than manservant. He offers Steed a frosty welcome, warning us to expect something unpleasant inside.

It is the glass-ceilinged plant room – which we will return to for the final scenes – that adds the avengerish, surreal atmosphere to the mansion. Naked female mannequins stand guard, with climbing plants their only attire. Steed doffs his bowler to them, warning one of them that "come autumn, I hope to see more of you." The comment, on every level, is wonderfully strange. The set is effectively bizarre, as the figures create a brooding presence, almost as if they are watching him/us. As a recurring leitmotif in *The Avengers*, they always seem to unsettle us. Equally effective is Steed's spying on the botanists through the glass doors, as the camera constantly switches between Steed's view and close-ups of his spying eye.

Steed's interview with Sir Lyle offers us more early hints of the plot's main strand. In passing Steed his brandy, Lyle draws connections between human/plant life:

"Man differs little from plant life. Liquid nutriment is vitally essential."

More female waxwork dummies – with real hair – decorate his office, Lyle drawing a polarity between the "passive, inanimate" figures and the living plants which "feel, perhaps even think." The disturbing sight of Lyle feeding his 'pet' Venus fly-traps offers another miniature fore-echo of what is to come. Steed cannot look at these hungry, "gourmet" creatures, closing his eyes before changing the conversation.

Hayers' interesting direction comes in to play again as Steed leaves. We catch Lennox's menacing face in Steed's rearview mirror, having just 'planted' something deadly on the driver's seat. These little touches from the camera transform the episode, adding an extra creative and playful layer.

There are a number of science fiction and ecology episodes in Season 4, including some which combine the two, such as *A Surfeit of H$_2$0*. Serious questions about the potentially destructive results of scientific research are raised, even if they are quickly dropped again or forgotten amidst the action-adventure. *Man-Eater of Surrey Green* takes the science fiction/ecology theme to its extreme as the Avengers move on to the episode's most atmospheric location, the abandoned Moat Farm.

The scenes set at Moat Farm cleverly contrast with each other. The initial one sees Steed and Mrs. Peel drive along a deserted country lane, arriving at a collection of charmingly dilapidated outbuildings: weather-boarded wooden barns, brick outhouses and rusting corrugated sheds, surrounded by nettle-strewn, neglected grass. The haunting music teases us, as does the tile dropped by a startled dove. However, there is nothing sinister lurking in the interiors. It is the mound outside which we are asked to focus upon. As Steed is forced to swap umbrella for agricultural fork, the scene moves from realism to surrealism with the uncovering of a skeleton in a space helmet.

The macabre discovery moves seamlessly into the following scene at the same location. The previous rural silence has been shattered. The farm is now a hive of activity, the courtyard populated by military personnel and vehicles, winching equipment and metal detectors, scientists with testing tables. On a superficial level, it instantly transforms the previously brooding atmosphere to one of action. Wing Commander Davies' space ship explanation is at once pure fantasy yet also chillingly surreal:

"Poor chap died...up there...alone...five thousand miles up in the cosmos...since, the ship and the body have been circling in orbit."

The arrival of the wonderfully enthusiastic and eccentric Dr. Sheldon enables the team to verify Mrs. Peel's theory that the creature which the space ship collided with was vegetable, rather than animal or mineral. Steed's praise is offered in a patronisingly teasing manner, reminding us that he is not always the egalitarian, feminist sharer of adventures: "Very observant of you, my dear." The interplay in these twinned scenes between realism/surrealism is fascinating, the rural, isolated setting at odds with the unearthly, bizarre discoveries:

Sheldon: Imagine a plant that could think...*think!*

It is the surrealism which often lacks a dramatic undercurrent in *Man-Eater of Surrey Green*. Conversely, the 'realistic' deaths of a labourer and Alan Carter are atmospherically, chillingly filmed. As the butler shoots the zombified agricultural worker with his double-barrelled shotgun, the television screen is covered with smoke, obliterating any sight of the killer. The visual effect is horribly real. In the following scene on Lyle's estate, Laura Burford watches impassively as her fiancé is electrified by the perimeter fence, his hands remaining glued to the barbed wire.

Emma Peel's dry humour lightens the mood in an episode with plenty of charm and wit. As Dr. Sheldon collects her deadly herbicide, Mrs. Peel warns Steed:

"She'd better be quick or we'll all be on the menu."

The scene closes with Steed emphasising the importance of wearing a hearing-aid; however, she now plays the nonchalant role. After all, "the plant's only *man*-eating!"

It is in the final ten minutes that *Man-Eater of Surrey Green* suffers, visually. Up until now, the writer and director have kept the giant plant under wraps, quite literally. As Steed, Emma and the elderly Dr. Sheldon enter Sir Lyle's surreal plant room, the sense of the creature covering the whole building, blocking windows and pressing down on the glass roof is effective, adding an uncomfortably claustrophobic feeling. However, the sight of its fat 'tentacles' dragging bodies away to be devoured does not work, neither on a dramatic nor a self-referentially artificial level. The images become ridiculous and it is left to Steed and Emma to provide the surreal spectacle.

Their fight with each other works on a number of levels. It upsets our sense of the correct order of things, forcing us to take sides. On an artistic level it is effectively shot, with their figures often foregrounded with vegetation which frames the images. On a comic level, the pauses to either pick up or tip over the herbicide container add a subtly silly element.

As the herbicide takes hold, the avengerish atmosphere is maintained by the strange sight of the mannequins crashing to the ground, rather than the sound of the man-eater screaming as it shakes furiously in its death-throes.

The episode loses its hold or grip on us when we are forced to see the plant close-up. The old adage of 'less is more' should have been adhered to here; perhaps even 'none is more'. In every other respect, *Man-Eater of Surrey Green* is an enjoyable, visually-striking episode, topped off with the sight of Steed and Emma relaxing on the hay bales of a tractor trailer, as the vehicle recedes along a deserted country lane towards that 'bright horizon'.

SILENT DUST

Minister: Kill the earthworm, Steed, and ultimately you kill everything. Soil...birds...animals...Man!
Steed: Fantastic!

One of the unique characteristics of *The Avengers*, particularly in Season 4, is the memorable story titles. They can instantly recall viewers to a specific episode. Many of these were discussed at length and re-worked between script completion and filming. *An Hour to Spare* became the far more mysterious *The Hour that Never Was*. *Strictly for the Worms* changed to the haunting *Silent Dust*. The fact that these titles were examined in such detail, as one might with a novel or one-off play, indicates that *The Avengers* was not simply light entertainment but individual works of art in which every detail was considered important. In his study of *Silent Dust*, *Le Monde des Avengers* webmaster Denis Chauvet offers an intriguing insight into the possible origins of the title:

"The title was surely inspired by *Silent Spring* which had been published in September 1962. This bestseller is often considered to have initiated the environmental movement in the West. In the book, the marine biologist Rachel Carson described the deadly consequences of pesticides (notably DDT) on the environment, more specifically birdlife; this phenomenon is directly alluded to in the episode's teaser. Carson even pointed the finger of accusation at the chemical industry."

If Chauvet is correct, this offers an interesting example of the series' ability to respond subversively to 1960s fears, engaging in the counhercultural politics of the period.

In my introduction I described the move from video-tape to film as liberating the show. Despite this new-found freedom, many of Season 4's early episodes are claustrophobically studio-bound; effectively so in the case of *The Murder Market*, *Dial a Deadly Number*, and *Death at Bargain Prices*. However, while both *The Gravediggers* and *A Surfeit of H2O* include memorable exterior scenes, *Silent Dust* is the first episode which takes full advantage of film, of the ability to use outside locations. It offers viewers a tongue-in-cheek take on a certain stereotypical rural Englishness and effectively mixes the real with the surreal.

The 'teaser' is a highly distinctive one, with not a human in sight. Images of birds feeding their young, accompanied by a gentle bucolic score, create a brief feeling of arcadia. However, this dramatically changes as the birds drop dead; one can already sense the influence of Hitchcock even before the gnarled, dead tree and the evil-looking jagged-tooth scarecrow produce a malevolent atmosphere. As the music becomes increasingly disturbing, the camera focuses in on the scarecrow which – like clowns, toys, puppets and stuffed animals – is an unsettling *Avengers* object.

The scene immediately afterwards returns us to arcadia. Despite the attractive, summer portrait of punting on a pretty river estuary, we retain the earlier unpleasant images. Nevertheless, in a sense we have, for the time being, left Hitchcock behind for a typically *Avengers* spoof. As the camera closes in on the boat we realize that it is Steed relaxing in blazer and boater under a parasol, with Mrs. Peel left to punt.

Steed: Tired?
Emma: Exhausted.
Steed: No stamina.
Emma: No comment.

The scene is witty but what are the gender dynamics which it employs? Steed as male chauvinist? Mrs. Peel as the dogsbody? Or is Emma being robustly treated as an equal/male, rather than the stereotypical 'delicate' (aka feeble) female? Despite Steed often using Emma Peel to perform the more unpleasant or humdrum tasks, they have a working relationship where – in terms of verbal dexterity and physical capability – he treats her as his equal, as we the viewers do. It was revolutionary in a television drama of the mid-1960s for a female protagonist to be portrayed as being physically and mentally able to (more than) match her male partner. Her ability to rival him in witty exchanges (and alcoholic consumption) emphasises this equality of the sexes.

Silent Dust is interesting in the ways it effortlessly weaves between realism and surrealism, often within the same scene. The Manderley sequence is an example of this. The writer, Roger Marshall, suggested that the 'exterior' shots be filmed in the studio: "An air of artificiality would *heighten* the atmosphere." On one level, the scene is naturalistic: the dead, silent landscape – resembling no-man's land – is effective, as is the explanation that 'Silent Dust' is the result of an experimental organo-chlorine fertilizer which has gone catastrophically wrong, creating the opposite effect:

Steed: Some fertilizer!
Minister: It went wrong. Instead of renewing – replenishing, it killed.
Steed: Best pesticide I've ever seen.

The dangers of scientists attempting to 'improve' nature, and thereby destroying the fragile eco-system, makes an interesting starting-point. This realism is undercut in a number of innovative ways. The hay-fever suffering minister seems more concerned with enforced late changes to his hockey team. When the pair swap their footwear due to the radio-active soil, they order (golf-like) shoes from what resembles an ice-cream van. These bizarre details take us away from the 'real', yet, as Marshall hoped, increase the atmosphere.

This constant interplay between realism and the surreal or bizarre applies to other characters. Quince, the birdwatcher, is a ridiculous caricature, an over-sized boy scout in a jungle outfit, whistle-warbler and constantly slipping pebble glasses. However, both his death – strangled by the tattooed ox-like Juggins – and the discovery of his corpse in an apple store are disturbingly real.

The scenes which take place in and around the dilapidated farmhouse also reflect this interplay. Emma Peel's nighttime visit is atmospheric, yet accompanied by the clichés of a full moon, hooting owl and a fleeing bat. When Steed is shot by the gamekeeper and hunted down while caught in a gin-trap, the drama is played straight. Yet the next time we see him we are taken inside his dream/nightmare where he is a sheriff from a Western film, surrounded by 'Wanted' posters for Omrod and Mellors. A moustached Mrs. Peel arrives as the 'Doc', slugging from a bottle of Red Eye and removing a giant bullet from his superficial wound. The oneiric scene is unimportant, irrelevant in terms of plot. Somehow that doesn't matter; it is simply part of the surreal fun and the playful disturbance of realism. It is another example of *The Avengers*' distorting mirror.

The guest characters are stereotypes, as others are keen to point out to us. Omrod tells us that the scrumpy-guzzling Juggins is a "bloodthirsty villain"; Omrod himself, in Peel's words, is a "local squire-type"; while Beryl Snow, Steed informs us, is the "horsey type". They are, paradoxically, both caricatures yet also completely believable. When Mrs. Peel comments about the absence of martlets, Omrod's casual, arrogant reply rings true:

"Really? I wouldn't know...Frankly, if you can't hunt it or shoot it – I'm not interested."

The verbal exchanges between Steed and the diabolical mastermind provide wit intermingled with menace in another example of interplay:

Steed: Birds are getting scarcer every minute.
Omrod: I hadn't heard.
Steed: You should ask your gamekeeper.
Omrod: Mellors?
Steed: Mistook me for a partridge.
Omrod: I'll speak to him. He ought to be more...
Steed: Accurate?
Omrod: Careful!

Omrod is a three dimensional 'type' but it is, of course, a role he is playing. He is an outsider/actor, playing the part of the squire. His hierarchical position in village life (and his friendship with Prendergast) is simply to ease his way into his master plan of holding the country to ransom. Once again we have a character that is both more and less than he seems.

Silent Dust is also intertextually playful. Some of the references to Shakespeare, Herrick, Wilde etc. add a further layer of meaning to the witty dialogue. "The temple-haunting martlet" (*Macbeth*) increases our sense of a disturbing atmosphere. Omrod and his henchmen are indeed the "unspeakable" (happy to kill off the country, county by county) in pursuit of the "uneatable" (Steed and Mrs. Peel). Other intertextual references are there to add a deliberate artificiality to the drama, as when Mrs. Peel first tells Steed about the gamekeeper: "Mellors? Not *the*...?"

If *Silent Dust* is a stylish, surprising *Avengers* gem, it also contains a very unavengerish detail, added by the production team before filming commenced. In the lead-up to the hunt, anti-hunt "cranks" (the production team's word) are placed outside the Stirrup Cup Inn, carrying notice-board banners: 'DOWN WITH BLOOD SPORTS'; 'BE KIND TO ANIMALS'; 'DOWN WITH VIOLENCE'. On one level this is simply a convenient device, allowing Steed to pick one of the boards up later – like a polo player – and attack Juggins with it. This enables the villain to be knocked out by the pacifist board in a moment of (arguably heavy-handed) ironic humour; this 'playful' violence contrasts with the 'real' violence of Juggins whipping Mrs. Peel. However, the detail goes against one of the unwritten *Avengers* rules: it brings a political/public reality into the private sphere of *Avengerland*, a world devoid of ordinary people, pedestrians, traffic and policemen.

The creation of exclusive places emptied of the normal or mundane is central to the otherness of *The Avengers*, and is crucial to the show's artificial, self-referential, atmospheric appeal.

THE HOUR THAT NEVER WAS

Steed: I promised you a quiet ride in the country.

The Hour That Never Was is an all-time favourite episode both with critics and 'fans' voting on online forums. From some points of view this is a surprise. There is a wafer-thin plot, the diabolical mastermind is not a memorable one, nor is it an episode with as much verbal wit as other Roger Marshall scripts. You could go as far as to say that it is a story in which very little happens. This observation, though, partly explains its iconic status.

With no one but Steed and Mrs. Peel seen on camera for over half the running time, it is the most experimental and unusual episode of the season. What it lacks in the way of plot or storyline it makes up for in terms of eerie atmosphere, thanks mainly to the innovative nature of both Marshall's script and the direction of Gerry O'Hara who – drawing on his background in film – set out to create a visual, filmic feast, rather than a television episode. The result was an extraordinary *Avengers*.

To understand how unique and remarkable *The Hour That Never Was* is, you almost need to re-watch it while jotting down a time map, appropriate for a story which revolves around 'stolen' time.

The running-time (without credits) is approximately 47 minutes. For the first 15 of these, Steed and Mrs. Peel are continuously on screen without (us) seeing another human being. Even then we simply see – from the Avengers' bird's-eye viewpoint in the RAF control tower – a man sprinting across the runway before being shot. No one else speaks until Steed encounters Hickey, the tramp, half-way through the episode. To a large extent the tramp – who I will return to – represents a diversion or sub-plot and the 'real' guest characters are not introduced until fifteen minutes from the end. My timeline is a crude one; nevertheless, it illustrates the daring nature of *The Hour That Never Was*, an episode which veers away from not only the *Avengers* formula but from that of any 1960s television series.

By reading a copy of almost any *Avengers* shooting script one can gain a reasonable impression of the television episode which evolved from it. In the case of *The Hour That Never Was* you hardly begin to understand the scenario until you watch it.

Director O'Hara described his first impression of the draft version as receiving the wonderful gift of a "visual" script (Optimum/Studio Canal DVD commentary). It is, paradoxically, both a static and constantly shifting narrative. Static, in the sense that all the exterior shots are in a single location: the agoraphobic, deserted airbase; constantly shifting because Steed and Mrs. Peel are on the move all the time.

The location itself – the fictitious RAF Hamelin – is as much a character as the humans themselves. The odd assortment of buildings and vehicles allows for a series of experimental shots through doors, machinery, in the reflection of standing water etc. The serendipity of finding an absurdly-shaped black outbuilding which mirrors Steed's bowler hat allows the latter to pause, acknowledge and salute it. The unconscious rabbit is filmed under the "roof" of an aircraft, providing the director with yet another "off the wall" (O'Hara's words) image. Steed and Mrs. Peel express their bewilderment about the mysteriously deserted airbase and the bizarre happenings:

Steed: Razors still running, petrol pumps gushing...
Emma: Ten thousand bottles of milk.
Steed: ...And thirty full grown men. All sane, highly trained, technical men. Suddenly up and dance away from...
Emma: From *Hamelin*!

Their words are both magnified and distorted by the (naturally) echoing hangar where the scene was shot, subtly changing their meaning. While any television drama is a co-creation of writer/director (plus actors, set designers etc.) this is even more evident than usual in *The Hour That Never Was*.

Even before the car crash, the 'teaser' sets up the *Avengers* interplay between the real and mundane on the one hand, and the surreal or bizarre on the other. We have the "serenity" of a Constable landscape interrupted by the "strange behaviour" (Mrs. Peel's words) of a dog chasing nothing across a country road.

The bleak, desolate airbase appears banal and uninteresting at first. Ordinary in every way apart from the fact that it is deserted. However, the "visual" storyline and direction allow everyday objects to become disturbing and/or surreal: the spinning front wheel of a bicycle, the overflowing petrol tank, and the abandoned milk crates.

Part of the surrealism comes from the sounds which puncture and punctuate the silence. The main one, of course, is the "strange whirring, electrical sound of a milk float". It fulfils a similar role to that of a sinister piece of music.

There is both irony and paradox in the fact that it is a mundane noise – heard on a daily basis – which disturbs us the most. Placed in a different spatial/mental context – an *Avengerland* – everyday objects or sounds can become unsettling: nodding dogs, stopped clocks, a milk float's whine.

The ultrasonic sound – emanating from the diabolical dentist's drill – transforms other ordinary objects into surreal, threatening ones: the intense rattling of the milk crates (in the case of Emma Peel);

the agitated rattling of the chains (for John Steed). Even the milkman's corpse on the float appears to be wriggling.

I described the anti-hunt extras in *Silent Dust* as being out of place in *Avengerland*. One might expect Hickey, the airbase tramp, to be a similarly inappropriate character. However, as his full name indicates, Benedict Napoleon Hickey is a wonderfully bizarre figure. Existing at the dustbin end of the RAF food-chain, he is the first speaking character Steed encounters, at exactly the halfway point of *The Hour That Never Was*. His archaic vocabulary — Dickensian words like "victuals" — and Pinteresque ramblings (e.g. his disapproval of stamp collectors) provide us with a humorous break from the increasingly disturbing plot. Ironically, his inability to answer Steed's questions directly sends the latter to breaking-point. Hickey is an absurd cross between Pinter's caretaker and Beckett's *Godot* tramps. If Hickey offers us welcome relief from the profound silence of the base, his presence increases the surreal atmosphere of RAF Hamelin. (As an interesting, factual side note Roger Marshall had Harold Pinter in mind when he created the tramp character, although he is unsure whether Pinter was ever invited to play the part.)

The absence of other characters and the physical isolation of Steed — after Mrs. Peel's disappearance — build an invisible wall of tension which eventually sees the impeccably cool Avenger snap. He uncharacteristically threatens the annoying (but innocent) Hickey before smashing a glass in the officers' mess.

There is a serious, psychological level to *The Hour That Never Was* in which we see how prolonged mental tension — maintained by the silence/whining milk float — can eventually lead to self-questioning. Mrs. Peel asks:

"Steed, we *did* see him, didn't we? He *was* here?"

Steed, in turn, on waking up back in his crashed car – and on re-entering the base – is forced to ask himself whether he is in a nightmarish dream. It is only the concrete presence of real objects – Mrs. Peel's watch, Hickey's corpse – which prevent him from losing his mind. This mental torture is kept up until the final scene of the episode.

As if to remedy the prolonged, serious drama of *The Hour That Never Was*, the final scene in the dentist's surgery – initially witty – soon collapses into both slapstick and the surreal. On finding Mrs. Peel strapped and gagged in the dentist's chair, Steed drily comments:

"Well – scared of dentists is one thing – but when they have to tie you to the chair…!"

Mrs. Peel's fight with two of Leas' henchmen is Batmanesque: sending one through the swing doors of the Casualty Department, the other flying through a wafer-thin set (corridor wall). The laughing gas finale completes this bizarre, tension-breaking finale.

The 'tag' scene continues the slapstick as the Avengers chase a speeded-up driverless milk float. This was neither the writer nor the director's choice, but a production decision. Although it angered television executives, O'Hara's response to it was "and why not?"

This open-minded approach to film-making sums up this revolutionary, atmospheric, risk-taking episode. Both the 'tag' ending and the mastermind's confession – "I could pretend it was my life's work…but it wasn't. It was an accident." – reveal how Marshall's *The Hour That Never Was* uses formula only to disrupt it from within. It is not surprising that actor Patrick Macnee was later to state that in the show's new and commercially-vital US television market it was with this episode – brought forward in the running-order to boost initially disappointing ratings – that "things started to happen" (cited by O'Hara).

If *Dial A Deadly Number* employs paired scenes to allow connections to be made both by the Avengers and the viewers, *The Hour That Never Was* uses a similar structural symmetry, this time to provide a (paradoxically) playful but sinister, dream-like atmosphere.

Steed experiences the car crash twice; he sneaks into the airbase via a back entrance on two separate occasions; he sees the spinning front wheel of a bicycle twice; finds the goldfish in the bowl dead, then alive; encounters Hickey alive, then dead. We, like Steed, are forced to question what we are seeing, until the obligatory laughter of the Nitrous Oxide. It is not only the characters who have the comic ending forced on them. The viewer is left breathless, having experienced an unsettling episode of subversive champagne. The traditionally passive consumer has been turned into an 'active' viewer; in *The Hour That Never Was* something special occurs. It is, arguably, the most iconic, groundbreaking episode in the entire series.

CASTLE DE'ATH

Steed: How deep is your moat?
Ian De'Ath: Deep enough for its purpose.

Castle De'ath has a unique charm about it, helped by the wonderful location of Allington Castle in Kent. The plot about the vanishing fish and a crisis in the British fishing industry is soon forgotten and the charm and fun of the episode lies in the red herrings – no pun intended – and the atmospheric setting.

Not a word is spoken in the teaser, which opens with the brooding loch landscape at dusk and the castle exterior. Against an aural backdrop of bagpipes, the hand-held camera takes us on a tour of the castle's interior, past suits of armour and eventually heading down into the dungeons where, finally, we encounter a human being, suffering on a medieval rack. At this point the bagpipes reach a crescendo. The areas which we have jerkily journeyed through will become familiar during the course of the episode, while the dungeons themselves will feature heavily. The title appears as we focus in on an Iron Maiden, racking up the dramatic tension in unison with Laurie Johnson's score.

The post-teaser scene sets up the polarity which will tease us throughout the episode: Ian De'Ath – the 35th Laird – is a traditional, fiercely-proud man, while his cousin, Angus, appears to be a modern playboy. It is Angus who has invited Mrs. Peel and 'Jock McSteed' to the castle, in an attempt to market Castle De'Ath as a tourist attraction. However, both Emma and we are led to believe that it is the Laird who wants the Avengers' visit literally terminated. The playfulness of the script encourages this belief but the signs that Angus is the diabolical mastermind are there from the start if we can read *Castle De'ath* against the grain. Angus' reckless firing of the crossbow in this scene warns us that he is a dangerous man yet we dismiss this as simply an example of his spirit or extrovert character.

In *Dial A Deadly Number* Steed publically, playfully tests Mrs. Peel's cover story of coming from Barbados. Here, Emma gets her own back as she interrogates him in front of the De'Aths:

Emma: You don't have a Scots accent.
Steed: I was carried south by marauding Sassenachs when I was a bairn.

Underneath the public conversations about castles and dungeons, Steed offers Mrs. Peel the private information that the dead frogman who the owners have been talking about "was four inches taller when he was dead than when he was alive." This immediately tells us that it is the same figure we saw being tortured on the rack in the teaser.

Much of the following storyline is wittily playful. Roberton spies on Steed who is testing the water in the moat: "Man, that's ridiculous. He's sailing a wee paper boat." Steed is happy to hide behind the jovial Jock McSteed, a historian tourist with the leisure time to fish and set paper boats on the water. He stirs things up, openly mocking the stereotypical castle ghost legends:

"The first thing a ghost learns is to walk through walls. It's a fundamental part of any self-respecting spirit's basic training."

The tongue-in-cheek comment echoes his earlier observation that "no self-respecting castle would be without [dungeons]." The light-hearted feel of the episode is maintained by the memorable scene in which Emma plays a set of miniature bagpipes while Steed does some impromptu Scottish dancing. Meanwhile, our suspicion of Ian De'Ath is cranked up by his ominous comments:

Steed: How deep is your moat?
Ian De'Ath: Deep enough for its purpose.

After Steed's four-poster bed is flattened by a deadly concrete ceiling which descends on his bowler, Ian comments that "perhaps we'll be more successful with another room." These seemingly dark observations are simply red herrings, preventing us from seeing the real mastermind who is under our very noses. Even the bed-crushing scene is turned into humorous material by McSteed:

"They've got a spot-on service here…tried to press my best shirt last night while I was still wearing it."

Scottish stereotypes abound in *Castle De'ath*, from the loch/castle setting, kilts and bagpipes to the porridge-eating scene in which Steed finds it impossible to eat his while the De'Ath cousins cover theirs with thick layers of salt. The look on Steed's face as the food is eaten adds humour while sending-up the traditional Scottish breakfast.

There is a cyclical nature to the episode, exemplified by Emma Peel's four visits to the dungeons. It is on her third trip down to the cobwebbed basement that she discovers the secret door to the submarine control room. The fact that this is hidden inside the Iron Maiden should have been obvious to us, given its prominence in the teaser. There is something symbolically fitting about Emma Peel using the Iron Maiden entrance to undermine the mastermind's plans.

After Ian De'Ath has politely asked Emma Peel to leave, apologising for his "apparent rudeness" – another clue that he is not the villain of the piece – we witness the fascinatingly shot scene in which the cousins confront each other, the darkly unreadable McNab standing between/behind them while their argument is played out. This becomes – in the atmospherically vast banqueting hall – an ideological debate as they argue their opposing sides of a "pompous" tradition versus "greedy" money-making polarity. It is appropriate that this medieval/modern argument takes place in an ancient castle, in the *olde worlde* setting of the hall, while down below Steed and Mrs. Peel are caught up in an attempt to wreck the modern technology of the submarine control room, (re-modelled from the set first seen in the bunkers of *The Town of No Return*.)

Despite Angus De'Ath's decidedly modern interests in technology and money, he is forced to fight McSteed in truly traditional Scottish fashion: with swords and shields in corridors, landing, and even on the banqueting table itself. It seems appropriate that his fatal demise is finally sealed in the medieval Iron Maiden, the portal between the ancient torture dungeons and the modern submarine pen. Emma Peel's change from a check, tartan-style outfit into her leather fighting gear is another visual reminder that *Castle De'ath* revolves around a traditional/modern binarism. This is lavishly illustrated in the tag scene as Steed and Emma veer off the main road in an amphibious car, driving/sailing across the loch against a never-changing backdrop.

The lightweight storyline or plot of *Castle De'ath* doesn't bear close scrutiny, yet this hardly matters in an episode which is wonderfully playful. We do not even feel cheated by the red herrings. The Scottish location – filmed in Kent – the castle setting and bagpipe music conjure up a sense of timeless adventure in which dungeon, rack, Iron Maiden, secret passageway and suits of armour help to create the noirish, atmospheric, brooding mood.

The episode lacks the cutting-edge surrealism and quirkiness of some of the season's classic episodes, but in terms of charm there is nothing better in Season 4. That this charm is based around faked, clichéd Scottish Gothic story-telling – Black Jamie's "ghost walks, playing the lament of Glen De'Ath on the bagpipes" – simply adds to the spectacle, rather than undermining it.

THE DANGER

MAKERS

Major Robertson: Once you've tasted danger, you're hooked. You need it.

The Danger Makers is witty and well-crafted but has become one of the forgotten episodes of Season 4. This is a great shame as underneath the well-polished veneer lies subversive humour and an interesting exploration of gender and stereotypes.

The plot of *The Danger Makers* is a realistic one, but with an avengerish twist: high-ranking military officers are suffering from the boredom of modern day warfare, or the lack of. Major Robertson laments the fact that wars are "rapidly becoming push button affairs" and that the 'military man' has become "defunct…obsolete…a dodo." The adrenalin of danger is seen as a deep-seated drug:

"Once you've tasted danger, you're hooked. You need it."

The response to a post-war safety-first culture is that men of action have resorted to "dicing with death" (in Mrs. Peel's words), in the form of radical risk taking, including Russian Roulette, grenade holding and the chicken running seen in the 'teaser'. The diabolical mastermind is a forces-based psychiatrist who utilizes this 'conditioned for danger' phenomena to encourage leading military figures to perform a series of tests: the "labours of Hercules". His grand plan is to steal the Crown Jewels.

This seems a relatively sane *Avengers* plot until one bears in mind some of the bizarre tests: crossing the Atlantic in a canoe, climbing the side of St. Paul's Cathedral etc. The 'inner temple' headquarters of the Danger Makers is at Manton House Military Museum. Its curator makes up for the 'straight' military men. She is a typically eccentric *Avengers* character who "lives in a dream world. She's recreating the Indian Mutiny in the Potting Shed."

The intriguing psychological narrative is undermined, first by Steed playing at being a psychiatrist and then Mrs. Peel who finds the couch so comfortable that it makes her sleepy. Yawning, she announces that "this is a very comfortable position."

Often, a darkly dramatic scene is set up, only to be challenged by humour. Steed makes Mrs. Peel worried that Robertson's chocolate box gift might be a "booby trap", before revealing that he simply wanted the wrapped ones for himself. When Robertson arrives to kill Steed, the dramatic tension is deflated by Steed's refusal to put his newspaper down and play the game:

Robertson: I've got to kill you.
Steed: Don't make too much noise about it will you?
Robertson: I said I've got to kill you.
Steed: My goodness me, British Tin down another point.

No sooner has the scene re-established the dark undercurrent than Steed cheats in their gun-grabbing game, reducing it to a ridiculous squabble between little boys. As Mrs. Peel arrives, the playful narrative is racked up a notch:

Steed: How did you get out?
Emma: I knotted some sheets and climbed out of the window.
Steed: Oh, that old thing.
Emma: Well, originality didn't seem important at the time.

Writer Roger Marshall uses the same device in *Death of a Great Dane/£50,000 Breakfast*. It is a popular *Avengers* device to playfully rework literary clichés which become freshly humorous once we are asked to poke fun at them, rather than take them seriously.

The Danger Makers even adopts a metafictional tone, coming close to breaking the 'fourth wall'. When Steed is being quizzed by Peters at Manton, he playfully threatens to expose both his cover and the show's fictional illusion:

Peters: You weren't in on that Liverpool job?
Steed: Unfortunately not.
Peters: No…I'd love to know how you got away with it.
Steed: So would I…
Peters: You can say that again…
Steed: I may have to.

People's preconceptions or stereotypical views about gender are often undermined in *The Danger Makers*. Major Robertson, awaiting a valuer for Woody Groves' effects, admits that he expected "a dusty old man leaning heavily on a gnarled stick". Instead, he finds himself involved in an intellectual conversation about phrenology and modern culture with Mrs. Peel. Steed imagines that the curator of the military museum will be an "old boy", "full of pepper and memories of the Khyber Pass." In place of his stereotype vision he encounters a lively, intelligent woman who refuses to be talked down to:

Adams: Women can also *serve* Mr. Steed, besides standing and waiting.
Steed: Women should never be kept waiting…and as for letting them *stand*.
Adams: You're mocking me.
Steed: My dear lady.
Adams: *Colonel* if you don't mind.

Steed's 'chivalry' is seen through for what it (sometimes) is: patronizing, condescending and chauvinistic.

Robertson is forced to accept that he has met his match in Mrs. Peel. The traditional machine-gun fire of a military base is replaced by a verbal equivalent of one-liners which provide the female lead with one of her best scenes in the series. The subject is the lack of danger and excitement in a 1960s culture of safety. Man is spiritually 'dead' according to Mrs. Peel:

Robertson: Dehydrated.
Emma: Sterile.
Robertson: Frightened.
Emma: Tasteless.
In unison: Atrophied.
Emma: Nine to five. Rushing home to his window box.
Robertson: Wrestling with the crossword…
Emma: Keeping up with the Jones's…
Robertson: Paying the next installments.
Emma: Life's for living…
Robertson: For living!

The humorously polished intellectual exchange is enough to convince Robertson to invite Mrs. Peel to join the exclusively-male Danger Makers. It is her cerebral powers – more than her sexual ones – which excite him. This type of witty dialogue would be less prevalent in the colour seasons.

The iconic 'test room' scene in which Emma Peel defeats the assault course of see-saws and high-voltage cables is played straight. Even then Peters' coughing fit threatens to undermine the dramatic tension, while paradoxically increasing it. We are unsure how to react. The final fight scene concludes with Colonel Adams calling "Tea up! Come and get it!" with a football rattle in her hand. She treats the soldiers as little boys and we are encouraged to do the same.

Even the 'tag' scene – in which Mrs. Peel asks Steed how he "stumbled on" the Danger Makers – leads to Steed playfully ridiculing the episode's "elementary plot".

The Danger Makers is a far more inventive, subversive episode than has been acknowledged by critics and fans. It deserves a place in this study of the champagne of Season 4. Emma Peel's 'concept of life' which she presents to Robertson could also be applied to the viewer's *Avengers* experience in this vintage season:

"A sense of challenge, change of scene – adventure, excitement – danger…!"

WHAT THE BUTLER SAW

Steed: It would not be exaggerating to say that the fate of...
Emma: The entire nation was in the balance?
Steed: That's just about it.

The teaser of *What the Butler Saw* offers a perfect example of the playfulness in *The Avengers* at this point in the show's evolution. We arrive mid-speech as a valet (Walters) explains to his master that with his job becoming "more dangerous" by the day he merits a pay rise. He appears nervous, as if he has shocked himself by speaking out, reminiscent of Oliver Twist asking for 'more'. The master – sat in an armchair – remains unseen by us, save for a distinctive ring on the little finger of his right hand. He rings a bell, at which point his butler (Benson) arrives. The light-hearted music is at odds with the action which follows, as the master takes a silencer from the proffered silver tray and kills the valet. This inexplicable act is sandwiched by the butler clichés of "You rang, sir" and "Will that be all, sir?" Once again we have an uneasy mix of the mundane and the menacing, the routinely real and the strangely surreal. How can a valet's job be "dangerous"? Why is the obsequious butler not shocked by the sudden, cold-blooded murder? Who is the unseen killer?

This sense of incomprehensible, conflicting events continues into the post-teaser scenes. First, the dead valet is thrown overboard from a rowing boat by the same, unseen man. If he is a master, why is he performing this task himself? We are then shown a barber's shop. With another client – covered by a towel – present, Steed begins two intertwined conversations with the (double agent) barber: a dramatically loud, public one in which the weather is discussed; a private, whispered one in which the selling of defence secrets is mentioned. The scene is at once ridiculous yet also strangely dramatic, as we see the distinctive ring for a third time, the barber silenced by a stabbing blade and having a shaving brush pushed into his mouth like a cork. We are only four minutes in but already we have two bizarrely executed murders.

The barber's suggestion that there are three possible suspects selling state secrets warns us to expect a typical *Avengers* episode in terms of formulaic structure. Initially, this proves to be the case as Steed visits all three, in three different disguises. Vice-Admiral Willows' home is straight out of an *Avengerland* fantasy, his waterside house resembling a boat, down to the finer details such as a ship's steering wheel, gas lamps and portholes in the front door. Steed – as the bearded Commander Red – gets into the spirit, arriving by boat, accompanied by suitably nautical music and announcing his arrival with an "Ahoy there!" Despite the presence of Benson, as soon as we encounter Willows we know that he is not the villain, even before he laments the disappearance of his usual manservant, Walters. There is a clichéd, heavy irony as he describes him as going AWOL: "jumped ship, fell overboard." Interestingly, this was where the dumping of Walters' body was originally planned to be shown, and one is left to wonder why it was brought forward.

As the anticipated triptych structure of the early plot reveals itself, Steed arrives at Brigadier Ponsonby-Goddard's house in a tank, the music still light-hearted but now recognisably military. Brian Clemens' script describes Steed's undercover character (Major White) as that of a caricature: "stiff upper lip, clipped speech and manner – rigid, 'proper' posture." As Steed waits to see Goddard, the scene becomes surreal, then absurd. First, his eyes are drawn to a life-size replica horse, with what appears to be a pale-faced mannequin sat on it in an old-fashioned uniform. Having affectionately patted the horse, Steed is then astonished – as we are – to see that the figure is real. In true *Avengers* style, Steed is then encouraged by the Major-General to play some war games with him, the fireside representing the West Ridge.

Brigadier: Father, I've told you before about playing around in here.
Major-General: Playing! *Playing?*
Brigadier: Manoeuvres then. Kindly confine your activities to the garden. And don't blow up the roses again! All right then – off you go!

In this strangely eccentric world, nothing is quite what it should be: butlers delivering silencers on silver trays, barbers acting as double agents, retired military men behaving like little boys. When the Major-General tells Steed that his son is a "traitor" we are left to wonder if there is any method in the madness; are they the ramblings of a senile old man? Is the Brigadier's early morning drinking the sign of nerves, or guilt? There are puzzling signs being playfully placed everywhere, daring us to interpret them. As Steed departs, he overhears another butler acting strangely, organising a nighttime *rendez-vous*. If Steed is baffled, then so are we; the opening ten minutes have been so odd that we doubt our ability to read between the lines.

The third and final part of the triptych opening almost inevitably sees Steed arrive at Group Captain Miles' residence in a helicopter. His undercover name is, of course, 'colourful' again: Squadron Leader Blue, taking the running joke into the genre of farce, in keeping with his giant moustache and the RAF marching music. Once again the house is decorated with themed props or toys, although this time Steed's over-the-top disguise is matched – quite literally – by the equally fruity-voiced, moustached Squadron Leader Hogg. The subsequent acronym-ridden conversation sees the slapstick reach an absurd crescendo, although the cycle has now been broken in that the randy Group Captain is absent.

The amusing sight of Steed hiding among the rose bushes while eavesdropping in the conservatory stylishly and seamlessly leads to the following scene in which it is a relief to find Emma Peel finally making her entrance, adding a more subtle touch to an episode which – it is already abundantly clear – will be 'played for laughs'.

Steed: Mrs. Peel, if a man's susceptibilities are to be strained to nerve-jangling breaking-point, if he's to be pushed to the very point of betraying Queen and Country, then who better than you to…
Emma: Vital you said?
Steed: It would not be exaggerating to say that the fate of…
Emma: The entire nation was in the balance?
Steed: That's just about it. Defence secrets are being sold to the…
Emma: Other side?
Steed: And it must be one of three people…an Admiral who gambles too much…a Brigadier who drinks too much…and a Group Captain who…A Group Captain.

The crisp dialogue offers us a knowing wink at the series' formulaic approach, while also demonstrating Mrs. Peel's weary or cynical attitude. The plot revels in the potential for red herrings, as well as its butcher/baker/candlestick maker structure. However, Emma Peel disrupts the formula, and adjusts Steed's sexist plan:

Steed: Shouldn't be too difficult to pick him up.
Emma: HE will come to ME.

Emma Peel is here living up to her carefully-created name, a woman with magnetic 'man-appeal'. Her carrying a rose cleverly connects to the previous scene. Has Steed offered her the flower in an attempt to win her over to his plan? It is a subtle touch amidst the less-refined humour.

Steed's moonlit arrival at the Brigadier's house offers us the first moment of genuine, straight drama. As he enters through the French windows, the toy horse is fore-grounded by the camera, offering us a warning before we see the mysterious ringed hand appearing on it. The scene is stylishly shot, the butler's dead body theatrically spread on the rug with a sword sticking out. The foregrounding of some spiked helmets again warns us that one will be used to attack Steed, allowing us to stay a split-second ahead of him while increasing the tension. After all, unlike Steed, we are powerless. The helmet fails to spear him but allows the villain to remain masked. The clever scene is completed by the odd sight of the Major-General in pyjamas and night cap playing the Last Post over the butler's corpse.

What the Butler Saw exemplifies the one-off, individual nature of each Season 4 episode. This is illustrated by the unnecessary but amusing short scene which follows, in which Emma Peel has driven out into "the middle of the countryside", in order to enjoy "a breath of fresh, country air" as she informs Steed on her car telephone. It is as if this mad caper itself needs a breather before galloping on. Her 'Operation Fascination' involves bombarding Miles with photographic images displaying her 'man appeal'. Laid low in his study with a hangover, her photos are everywhere. Moving on to the military bar, her face even appears on his drink mat. The humour is heightened by the half-hidden Steed who is encouraging Mrs. Peel to speed up her romance campaign. The arrival of two female officers increases his concern, before Emma's wonderful, sexually-confident retort: "Competition? What competition?" The moment is a gently funny highlight of the season. As Mrs. Peel lowers her sunglasses, Miles is instantly smitten and Emma shuts the partition bar door, placing Steed outside the spectacle, a joke which will be reworked later on at Miles' love nest.

The noticeboard for the Butlers & Gentleman's Gentlemen Association is a forerunner of an *Avengers* tradition of amusingly snobbish organisations which runs throughout the filmed era, their motto typical of what will become a regular gag: 'BETTER BRIGHTER MORE BEAUTIFUL BUTLING'. Twenty minutes in and we are back in the elegant room of the teaser, a ringed hand tapping the arm of the same chair. The ringing of the bell and the subsequent arrival of Benson teases us, offering the (irrational) fear that Steed will be dealt with in the same way as Walters. To add an extra twist, the mastermind appears to have been finally revealed: surprisingly, it is the Group Captain's butler, Hemming. The subsequent conversation playfully sends up the language of domestic service, Hemming praising Steed for his "fine grasp of the vernacular". There is a delicious humour in the idea that Steed's "general demeanour" makes him a promising candidate for 'butling'.

The subsequent training fore-echoes that of the nannies in *Something Nasty in the Nursery* and the window cleaners of the Classy Glass Cleaning company in *Super Secret Cypher Snatch*. Indeed, from many points of view this episode has the comic-strip approach of the colour era, demonstrating how some of the late-season episodes were moving towards an increasingly bizarre *Avengerland*. The scenes involving shoe polishing, ironing and tray holding provide an echo of the early triptych structure, although they also represent amusing 'padding' at the halfway point of the episode. On another level, there is a clever self-referentiality at play as Hemming and Steed rehearse lines for a potential butler/master scene. On a final level, they should have us questioning whether Hemming really is the diabolical mastermind. After all, if he is the arch-villain then why is he bothering to train Steed?

What the Butler Saw is in a constant state of inner conflict, veering between silly and subtle, in common with a number of Brian Clemens episodes written towards the end of the monochrome era. The three high-ranking officers who were Steed's original suspects are seen discussing high security matters inside a zipped-up plastic bag, a new security ruling to foil bugging devices. Whether the image works or not is a matter of personal taste. Certainly, it tests the series' boundaries.

Hemming's murder takes us back to square one in terms of uncovering the identity of the mastermind. These scenes at the butler training academy are atmospherically shot by Bill Bain, with Hemming shadowed by Benson and, later, Steed's reappearance first indicated by the silhouette of his bowler, umbrella and upper body on a wall, before we see him adjusting his hat in an upturned, gleaming iron. If the storyline prefigures the cartoonish colour era then the more stylish touches remind us that we are still in the monochrome season. The sight of Hemming's corpse, seen through the glass porthole of the industrial washing machine, adds a chillingly surreal touch. Coupled with Benson's arrival, armed with a silencer, the dramatic tension rises but both Steed and the viewer are being teased. The discovery that his butler references are forgeries has allowed him into the villain's circle, rather than signing his death warrant. Benson's earlier remark that he will "attend to" Steed is a diabolically playful one, encouraging us to head down another false trail.

Steed's arrival as Miles' new butler allows the episode to return to its most natural tone, that of an almost slapstick, light-hearted humour, Steed rising above his new station to suggest that "Modom [Mrs. Peel] looks the cat's whiskers". Miles' 'master switch' instantly turns the room into a love nest: curtains drawn, soft lighting, smoochy music, chilled champagne at the ready. Even Miles himself has been transformed, wearing a silk lounging jacket. It is almost as if *The Avengers* has collided with a *Carry-On* film. The scene becomes manically absurd, as Emma desperately tries to avoid Miles' embraces by asking questions about his art collection and butler Steed regularly interrupts to demand if he should serve champagne, dinner etc. In a further twist it turns out that 'Casanova' Miles is a role he is tired of playing, relieved to enjoy a cup of tea, a chat and a board game instead.

When the plot is finally unravelled – miniature tape recorders stitched into the officers' uniforms; the bitter barman/dishwasher Sergeant Moran the unlikely mastermind – what we are left with is a strangely satisfying episode. Great credit should go to the strong guest actors: John Le Mesurier is wonderful as the obsequious, villainous butler – recalling his memorable role as the corrupt doctor in *Mandrake* – Thorley Walters plays the part of Hemming with style, Denis Quilley is hilarious as the Casanova officer, while Kynaston Reeves plays the batty, eccentric, retired Major-General with aplomb. As was so often the case, the strength of the supporting cast in this episode is a key element in the success.

At times, *What the Butler Saw* is subtly stylish, never more so than in the fight finale between Emma and Moran, a scene employing the butlers' doors – a wonderfully artificial set-within-a-set – but sometimes this subtlety makes way for farce, anticipating the comic-strip approach of many of the colour episodes. Brian Clemens' story feels as if it is caught between two worlds: the noirishly fantastic monochrome world of Emma Peel and the colourful, cartoonish era which would replace it. It is a highly enjoyable, daring romp, but one which arguably lacks the dark, dramatic touches of earlier Clemens episodes. As the antithesis of –

or antidote to – the disturbing *The House That Jack Built*, perhaps this doesn't matter; after all, *What the Butler Saw* adds yet more variety to this excitingly unique season. As the punch-line of the tag scene demonstrates – "the butler did it!" – it is happy to play with clichés, unwilling to take itself too seriously.

THE HOUSE THAT JACK BUILT

Keller: The mind of a machine cannot reason. Therefore it cannot lose its reason...Its mind has no breaking point. But *your* mind...

Occasionally, the Emma Peel *Avengers* episodes drop the light-hearted, witty 'froth', allowing the dark, dramatic undercurrent to bubble to the surface. They retain the quirky, surreal elements, but the result is unsettlingly sinister, as is the case in *The Joker*, *Epic* and *Murdersville*. However, Brian Clemens' *The House That Jack Built* is (arguably) far more terrifying than any of these. A sadistically imaginative script, some experimental direction and a psychologically disturbing, psychedelic set combine to create a nightmarish episode. *The Avengers* frequently draws upon the gothic horror genre of the remote country house 'trap', but here the visual result is uniquely, creatively unpleasant.

The teaser, initially, offers us a realistic scenario as an escaped prisoner is pursued by guards and bloodhounds. Two stone lions – guarding the front door of a remote country house – offer us a playful example of delayed decoding. As the convict, Burton, breaks in, he/we are convinced that the house is empty, which, in a sense, it is. The stuffed owls provide the first unsettling image. However, it is the obviously artificial (film projection) lion attacking him which we close/freeze on as the title appears on the screen.

The isolated country house may be a popular *Avengers* location, but here it becomes a claustrophobic set-within-a-set, or rather a series of them. However, before this is revealed, we have the bizarre 'key' scenes. First, Steed's own film-developing ends up with his holiday snaps – realism – stamped with a surreal key image, offering us a fore-echo of later events. Then, as Mrs. Peel heads off along deserted country roads, the surreal sight of Withers/Pongo – dressed as an over-sized boy scout – adds a disconcerting, absurd humour as he races down the hillside before stepping out in front of her speeding sports car:

Emma: I might have killed you.
Pongo: The speed you were going – the stopping distance of this car is one hundred and forty-seven feet – allowing for average reflexes – I positioned myself one hundred and fifty feet away.
Emma: Very mathematical of you.
Pongo: I am a very mathematical person.
Emma: You are also very stupid.

During the subsequent car journey we are left to wonder about Emma Peel's last comment. Is Withers/Pongo simply a ridiculous, comic figure? As he stares at the dangling key, the camera focuses on his bare legs which he caresses. It is a potentially sexual image, and Emma Peel/we are understandably uncomfortable. His observation that this is "very pleasant countryside...so quiet, empty" is at odds with both his peculiar behaviour and the mechanically-changing road signs. The tension increases as a 'ROAD CLOSED' sign bangs down behind them; the music becomes disconcertingly strange as Emma Peel heads up the drive towards the house we saw in the teaser.

From now on, the film will move between the interior 'trap' of the house and Steed's journey along the country lanes, with the added problem of having to read the road signs 'against the grain'. Steed is the knight – without shining armour – attempting to rescue the far from helpless damsel, *The Avengers* playing with the fairy tale genre as both Steed and Mrs. Peel acknowledge in the final minutes.

Don Leaver's direction helps to create the dark, dramatic atmosphere inside the house. When Emma Peel sees the stuffed owls from the teaser, we now get a close-up of their dark, unreadable eyes: first both owls, then one, lastly just the one eye which almost takes up the entire screen. A bewildering range of sounds shatter the silence: a music box, a phone ringing, a lion growling. There is no sense of connection and it will be up to Emma Peel to decode the signs. As she answers the old-fashioned phone, her expression offers a weary, disbelieving, self-referentially theatrical look.

The surrealism takes full control once the clichéd hallway – suit of armour, portrait with seemingly moving eyes etc. – disappears, replaced by a psychedelic set. Brian Clemens' original script offers a detailed description:

"In the middle of this central area is a perpetual motion machine. This area is like the hub of a wheel – and the spokes are corridors running off to blackness…The corridors are painted black and white with a jagged crazy pattern… weird, distorted look."

What are we to make of this set? It is, in a sense, a visual tease, as it serves no purpose other than to test Emma Peel's ability to 'keep her head', as the sets shift and force her to question what is 'real' and what isn't, a question we are frequently forced to ask ourselves in *Avengers* episodes. The set may be visually striking but it is brought alive by the camera work: as Emma Peel heads down an almost *Alice in Wonderland* spiral staircase, we follow the floor's spiral pattern, both to indicate her movement and add a sense of an almost drug-induced trip. As rooms move and/or are replaced by sets of themselves – the windows now boarded up – the sets become psychedelically surreal, rather than simply nightmarishly odd.

The use of Emma Peel's 'thought voice' adds an effectively strange extra layer to the mind games played by the late Keller. Her stopping of the moving rooms reveals to her/us their artificiality as they become stuck mid-change. As Brian Clemens had hoped, the visual effect "is not unlike being behind a studio set or in the wings of a theatre." The artificiality increases the sense of surreal fear, rather than reducing it. What are we to make, for example, of Emma Peel cutting through her giant photographed face and then stepping through it, moments later coming back to take a double take? Clemens describes it as "a disturbing image". We might read it as the triumph of the 'real' over surreal, manufactured representation.

As in *The Joker*, the plot revolves around "a pitting of wits" between the house/mastermind and Emma Peel. However, the theme of 'perfect' automation versus 'imperfect' human reasoning recalls *The Cybernauts*:

Keller: The mind of a machine cannot reason. Therefore it cannot lose its reason…Its mind has no breaking point. But *your* mind…

The sadistic scheme has at its symbolic centre or core the 'suicide box', while the mad prisoner – who has, ironically, swapped one cell for another – offers living proof that the house trap can drive its victims insane. Emma Peel's victory is not simply an obligatory part of the show's formula. It represents the thinking, reasoning human's defeat of the unchangeable, programmed, soulless automaton, once again displaying *The Avengers*' unease with the 1960s technological revolution.

The maddening, psychedelic hub; Keller's preserved corpse sitting in its chair in a glass prism; the suicide box; the dark beady eyes of the owls; the 'late Emma Peel' exhibition; Burton's nursery rhyme singing, his mad eyes staring at Mrs. Peel/us, all connect to create a disturbing visual feast.

As Steed and Emma cycle away towards that bright horizon, the formulaic happy ending fails to lift the gloomy darkness we have been encased in. It is impossible to define/confine *The Avengers* as 'light entertainment' on viewing *The House That Jack Built*; if Keller's house represents an intellectual puzzle then so too does *The Avengers* in its monochrome filmed episodes. It is simply the absence of wit and charm – the champagne fizz – which prevents this episode from being a 'classic' one.

HONEY FOR THE PRINCE

Hopkirk: A fantasy perhaps?
Emma: No thank you…I haven't yet exhausted reality.

My study of the 'subversive champagne' of Season 4 did not originally include *Honey for the Prince*. It is an engaging, delightful episode for the season to close with, but I omitted it simply because it lacks a dark, dramatic undercurrent. Hit-man Vincent East offers us the odd chilling moment and Arkadi is a memorable mastermind with an authentic edge to him, but in every other respect genuine dramatic conflict is absent. However, I now feel that I was wrong to exclude this episode. It *is* subversive, particularly in the way it playfully erodes the realism/fantasy polarity and exposes *The Avengers*' own fictionality.

We need to begin by placing *Honey for the Prince* within the context of the season and series as a whole, before discussing the episode's radical, innovative content. Some of the early Season 4 episodes like *The Murder Market*, *Dial A Deadly Number* and *Death at Bargain Prices* have one foot in the previous, studio-bound Mrs. Gale era. In contrast, *Honey for the Prince*, as the final episode in the season, has at least one foot in the following colour season. The cameras were waiting on the set to film the *Strange Case of the Missing Corpse*, a colour promotional trailer, aimed at the all-important US market. The trailer spells out the show's formula in simple terms and hints at the (arguably) less sophisticated approach which it would be taking in Season 5. *Honey for the Prince* itself has some of the feel of the cartoonish colour *Avengerland*. When Steed fights with Vincent East in George's office, he throws him out of an upper-floor window yet East escapes unscathed. Steed's comment – "Well I never!" – warns us that reality is being left even further behind as *The Avengers* reaches another crossroads in its evolution.

Characters like Ponsonby Hopkirk and B. Bumble of the Honey Shop are the types of frantically over-the-top eccentrics who will populate the colour seasons, as the 'quite, quite fantastic' begins to wrestle control of the show's real/surreal interplay. When Hopkirk tells Steed that "we will create your fantasies and let you live them" he is speaking as much for the viewers' evolving *Avengers* experience as he is for his Arabian Nights-inspired bureau. *Honey for the Prince* is, on one level, as much about *The Avengers*' own recipe for success — and its increasing interest in a radical self-referentiality — as it is about its individual storyline.

"As a boy I was fascinated by the tales of the Arabian Nights. I would dream of living in that exotic era...then one day I thought why dream? Why not make my dream a reality?...A matter of the right décor...the right atmosphere...a few tricks."

When Hopkirk introduces Steed to the QQF it reveals how playful *Honey for the Prince* is. His comments are, of course, a fantasy themselves. Hopkirk has not transformed 'dream' into 'reality'. He has simply provided a three-dimensional fantasy experience to supplement or supplant his clients' daydreams. Hopkirk's QQF games require a willing suspension of disbelief, ending with the fantasy's climax caught on a (gun-shaped) camera: a 'real fantasy' captured as a 'fantastic reality'.

The QQF's aim of creating the right ambience through décor, atmosphere and "a few tricks" mirrors the aim of *The Avengers*' writers, directors and set designers. If the clear connection isn't obvious enough to the viewer, it is then spelt out by Hopkirk when he suggests a fantasy role for Steed:

"a secret agent...ideal for you...licensed to kill — pitting your wits against a diabolical mastermind. Make a change from your everyday humdrum existence wouldn't it."

Steed's 'real' role as an Avenger is playfully exposed and/or reduced to that of a fantasy, the script revealing and revelling in its fictionality.

If we rewind to the 'teaser', this immediately introduces us to the episode's thematic concern with fantasy and self-referentiality. The Arabian Room of the QQF is a set-within-a-set, a series of props designed to excite and intrigue. The clients, like us, arrive expecting to be plunged into an alternative, fantastic world.

Realism is occasionally allowed in to offer interplay with surrealism and fantasy. In the 'teaser' the genie's lamp — one of Hopkirk's proudest props/tricks — ushers forth a deadly, machine-gunning hit-man. Amidst the elaborate Arabian doorways, vases and a stuffed bear, it is a sudden, violent, momentary intrusion of reality. Later, Hopkirk's rehearsal for East's fantasy will be terminated as the killer replaces the camera gun with an all-too-real one. Even then, the murder is played for its (darkly ironic) humour rather than straight drama. Reality is not allowed to establish itself.

If the QQF clients want to escape the drudgery of work for individually-packaged fantasies, the Barabian Prince is also keen to explore fantasy, transforming his palace's reception rooms into a cricket match, and thereby briefly escaping the grim reality of his 320 mothers-in-law. This brings me on to an area of *Honey for the Prince* which some critics and fans have centred on. There is a suggestion that alongside Mrs. Peel's (in)famous dance of the seven veils, there is a veiled critique of the Barabian harem, with its corridor of bedrooms for all his wives resembling prison cells, and the roster organised to satisfy the Prince's renowned sexual "ardour". I am not convinced. *Honey for the Prince* is light-hearted and it simply isn't avengerish to offer didactic criticism of political ideas or cultural customs. Equally, the storyline of governments providing military protection in return for oil concessions is simply a plot device mentioned in passing and soon forgotten. This movement away from heavily-plotted/researched scripts is part of the *Avengers* evolution. As I've already suggested, the subversion comes from the constant desire to undermine the establishment of realism in the episode. It is left to Mrs. Peel – unhappy at playing the belly-dancing role – to fight against this suppression:

Hopkirk: A fantasy perhaps?
Emma: No thank you…I haven't yet exhausted reality.

Once again the dialogue could be talking about the *Avengers* itself. As I observed in my introduction, the show was not created but evolved. It was now moving towards a colourful fantasy era but had not yet abandoned reality. The two would continue to offer us a fascinating and constant interplay. This conflict is still being negotiated in the 'tag' scene as Steed and Mrs. Peel ride a magic carpet…situated on a car. The 'reality' of the flying rug is another fantasy. *Honey for the Prince* demonstrates that *The Avengers* had moved on from semi-realistic plots to something far more bizarre.

Honey for the Prince allows the series to examine and explore itself both as concept and genre. It forces us, once again, to question what we are watching. In terms of exposing its own fictionality, this would reach a controversial climax in Brian Clemens' *Epic*. Here, though, the mood is far gentler. *The Avengers* at the end of Season 4 was offering an extraordinary televisual experience. Whether or not *The Avengers* 'in color' was quite, quite as fantastic in terms of artistic quality, innovation and variety is another, highly subjective matter…for the second section of this book.

EMMA PEEL 'IN COLOUR'

I have stated that *The Avengers* was a series with the ability to amuse and disturb simultaneously. In my introduction I suggested that by 1966/7 it had peaked, artistically:

there was a tendency to veer towards a simplified, psychedelic, colourised *Avengerland* in which subtlety and wit were often replaced by a cartoonish self-referentiality. It was vibrant and visually stunning but had, I would argue, lost some of its innovative zest. The decision to rework (or simply repackage) a number of successful episodes from previous seasons suggests that some of the earlier creative energy had been lost. (*Subversive Champagne*, pp. 15-16)

What emerges in the colour Peel era (1966-1967) is more unstable, less reliable: the remade Mrs. Gale episodes, unsurprisingly, are successful, but far too many others are simply formulaic, derivative or take eccentricity to the point of silliness, with little in the way of plot or dark, dramatic undercurrent. One or two are dull, lacking the required 'froth'. However, there are also some fantastic, surprising and radically innovative episodes, many of which would simply not have worked as well in monochrome. An episode such as *Something Nasty in the Nursery* is gloriously colourful, luxuriating in its Technicolor world and taking full advantage of it. Mrs. Peel's outfits suit the glamour of colour, be it her pea-green jacket in *Epic* or her purple jump-suit in *Murdersville*. Steed, somehow, always looks more elegant – almost timeless – in monochrome.

The interplay between realism and a surreal *Avengerland* is still there – much of the time – even if there is often a stronger pull towards a heightened surrealism (at the expense of realism and/or plot). Sometimes this provides us with a *more* disturbing, savage, even sadistic experience, as in *Murdersville*. This might be seen as a positive or a negative sea-change, depending on one's personal preferences.

The shift in style and emphasis of *The Avengers* between Series 4 and 5 is perhaps demonstrated – albeit crudely – by the different approach of both the writer and the *Avengers* team when dealing with essentially the same subject: *The Cybernauts/Return of the Cybernauts*. The original has a complex, intellectual debate at the heart of its storyline and is cleverly plotted with a string of red herrings. The sequel is less subtle, but effectively brutal, as the late Dr. Armstrong's brother fantasises about a "rhapsody of suffering" for Steed and Mrs. Peel. The basic idea is a chilling one and Peter Cushing's performance is thrillingly, cunningly evil. (The ability of *The Avengers* to attract top guest actors – thanks to its cult status – is a hallmark of Seasons 4 and 5 and a key ingredient of its success). The two-way mirror is a clever device, allowing the tension to rise at a key moment: Emma, carefree, as she plays with her hair while the three scientists study her, plotting her 'living death'. The scene in which Mrs. Peel helps Steed recover from a cybernaut chop – "How's the head?"; "What head?" – is later reversed, using the same dialogue. It is playful, but also reminds us of the closeness of the Steed/Peel partnership. The episode *is* memorable, thanks to some fine acting by the lead actors. There is also a wonderful line from Mrs. Peel, one of my all-time favourites, thanks partly to its delivery:

Beresford: Surely Steed can handle this alone?
Mrs. Peel: He could but I mustn't let him find out.

However, the episode, like so many in Season 5, is 'uneven'. There are the ridiculous scenes involving Rosie, the 'dumb blonde' secretary who is turned on by being hit by the cybernaut. It is a crude, sexist attempt at humour which is unforgiveable on so many levels. Although, as with all the 'glorious Technicolor' episodes, it looks great, there are some lazy continuity faults: Steed arrives at Beresford's on a dark evening but the scene is shot in bright daylight. To make matters worse, it is not even him – or a decent look-alike – driving the Bentley. *Return of the Cybernauts* relies too heavily on the success of the original, without reinvesting it with enough humour and subversive style. After the unforgettable experience of 'tangling' with a cybernaut, are we really expected to believe that Steed and Mrs. Peel do not immediately recognise the telltale signs of its return at the first crime scene? The sequel even (unnecessarily) recycles some of the footage from the original episode. It is a decent episode, but not nearly as good as it could have been, an epitaph for the season as a whole.

Thankfully, the larger number of disappointing episodes, paradoxically, makes the re/discovery of the ones which do 'work' even more exciting and rewarding. The aim of this smaller, second section of my book is to examine how *The Avengers*' Emma Peel colour era was still capable of shifting the boundaries of audience expectation – what I term its 'constant interplay' – defying both genre classification and our desire for closure and simplicity. The following chapters centre on individual episodes from Season 5. They cover a period which cannot be described as the pinnacle of the series' artistic achievement yet where the best episodes force the viewer to consider the very nature of television drama. What are we to make of an episode such as *Epic* with its brutally playful self-referentiality? Part of *The Avengers*' evolution/revolution is the disconcerting experience of watching films which reveal their own artificiality. In colour we often find ourselves confronted by mild eccentricity but also, sometimes, encounter something genuinely experimental.

The American television market was now having a profound effect on the product it was buying and funding. As David K Smith observes:

To satisfy the American market, the show itself was 'tweaked'. Emma Peel's 'strong' personality traits were toned down...Emma employed high-tech Karate in the monochrome episodes ...considered too 'unladylike'...the fighting mode of choice for the color season became graceful Kung Fu...Even the dialog was 'Americanized'...It seemed as if the very thing that made the show unique – its patent Britishness – was being compromised. (*The Avengers Forever!*)

If *The Avengers* was becoming Americanised, then parodying or playing up its Englishness is, paradoxically, part of this. (There are signs of this, of course, in previous seasons with Steed's Edwardian dress and bowler hat). The rough edges of the powerful female lead – previously groundbreaking in the cases of both Cathy Gale and Emma Peel – are smoothed over in Season 5.

Despite these problems, the colour Peel season provides us with a number of impressive – occasionally remarkable – episodes. Most of these come mid-season or late on. Season 5 is sometimes seen as two seasons, due to the enforced production break for financial reasons. This allowed for a creative re-think and, as filming resumed, there were some far more 'even' episodes made, including *Death's Door*, *You Have Just Been Murdered* and the excellent, iconic *Murdersville*. The sets were always fabulous – including an inventive, colourful P.U.R.R.R. cat sanctuary in *Hidden Tiger* – and the series maintained that distinctly avengerish look.

Experimental episodes such as *Epic* and *Murdersville* demonstrate that when the show took risks, genuine innovation provided an unsettling, disturbing experience which pushed the films well beyond traditional genre.

I referred earlier to the importance of the US market and how this affected both the style and content. Before one bemoans this outside interference, one needs to remember that by now it was American dollars which were keeping the show going:

With no further orders forthcoming from the US, it all came to an abrupt end in February 1969. The irony is that, had it not been for the US, there might never have been a color Emma Peel season, because the UK never ordered any episodes after the Emma Peel monochromes! And so the country that kept it alive, the US, also killed it, while the country that gave birth to it, the UK, orphaned it. (*The Avengers Forever!*)

As always with *The Avengers*, everything is both more and less than it seems, including its history. No wonder I state in my conclusion that "at the heart of *The Avengers* is a series of terminal paradoxes."

It is only by exploring a number of the episodes from the Emma Peel colour era (1966-1967) that one gains a sense of the 'uneven evolution' which took place within this short period. I return readers to the closing words of my introduction:

By the time I reach my conclusion we can begin to reflect on the extent to which *The Avengers*' use of recurring thematic concerns, leitmotifs and images undermined the sexual and textual politics of the kitchen-sink drama which it had gradually broken away from. Only then can we evaluate whether the show maintained the necessary substance to match its undoubted style. Was it simply froth and charm, or did it manage to be both evolutionary and revolutionary? Does it deserve its iconic status and my tag as '*subversive* champagne'? (*Subversive Champagne*, pp. 20-21)

Season 4 demonstrated that *The Avengers* often takes us well beyond formula, but within a formulaic structure. This structure was clearly set out and – in colour – was only tweaked in minor ways, such as the 'Mrs. Peel, we're needed' post-teaser tag which would be dropped after the mid-production break in Season 5. The early Season 5 episodes luxuriate in their new colour cloth, but tend to substitute formulaic for formula. Too often they lack the sense of individual films which had made so many of the monochrome episodes stand out.

The opening episode, *The Fear Merchants*, has an excellent premise – re-used with far more style in *You Have Just Been Murdered* – but it lacks the necessary plot or substance to profit from this. *The Bird Who Knew Too Much* and *The See-Through Man* mistake silliness for quirkiness. *The Living Dead* is a dull, poor person's *James Bond*. There is plenty of style, froth and humour in *From Venus With Love*, *Escape in Time* and *Never, Never Say Die*, but the scripts again – in my opinion – lack innovative substance and/or plot.

Hidden Tiger is the first inventive colour episode, with its memorable cat headquarters, the 'mad eccentric' Cheshire lapping up his milk and a clever, simple plot. It comes close to the tag of subversive champagne. However, the episode does not really get going until we reach the P.U.R.R.R. headquarters half way through. In contrast to *Return of the Cybernauts*'s sexist 'dumb blonde' secretary, we get the welcome role reversal in *Hidden Tiger* of Mrs. Peel coming to the rescue of the tied-up Steed.

It took a typical piece of *Avengers* serendipity to bring us a genuinely innovative colour episode…

EPIC

ZZ von Schnerk: This will be my ultimate masterpiece...A compendium of all my films...a picture with passion, with horror, with danger...and with Mrs. Peel in the lead.

According to writer Brian Clemens, the origins of *Epic* lay in a lack of finances, something which would eventually halt production for several months:

"It began, in a sense, because we had a budget problem. We wanted to save making too many sets…so I said 'OK, we'll just use the studios we're in'."

As with many of Clemens' comments, one needs to take this with the proverbial pinch of salt. I doubt *Epic* was considerably cheaper than other studio-based episodes such as *Escape in Time*. However, the result was a startlingly self-referential episode which goes well beyond the playful approach seen in Season 4. Clemens describes *Epic* as "a spoof on making films". I think we can take this a step further and call it a spoof on making an *Avengers* film.

The plot is fairly simple. A failing film producer/director kidnaps Mrs. Peel in order to use her as the reluctant star in a "downbeat movie", *The Destruction of Emma Peel*. Employing a couple of ageing, failing film stars, the 'real' movie is a patchwork quilt of film genre scenes: the ancient Classical world, Western, Great War Trenches, Gangster-land and Horror converge, with Mrs. Peel to be killed off in the climactic scene. With hindsight, this 'genre spoofing' offers us a fore-echo of the Season 6 episodes in which *The Avengers* re-uses established film genres such as Western, Conan Doyle-style detective fiction and fin-de-siècle Ripper Victoriana.

However, ZZ von Schnerk's wish to cast Emma Peel in the lead role immediately collapses *The Avengers*' fragile 'fourth wall'. Attracted by her "animal vitality", he offers us a succinct summary of Peel's attractively complex character:

"A woman of courage…of beauty…of action. A woman who could become desperate and yet remain strong…a woman who could become confused yet remain intelligent…A woman who would fight back…but yet remain feminine."

We find ourselves plunged into a surreal world where Emma Peel wakes up on a replica set of her flat which is – of course – the very same place, simply with the pretence of realism removed. *Avengers* leitmotifs – such as the interconnected wedding/funeral imagery – are literally flung at Mrs. Peel and these scenes are effectively subversive. A confetti-storm in a churchyard transforms seamlessly into an autumnal graveyard; wedding bells are replaced by funereal ones as illuminated headstones – 'R.I.P Emma Peel' – offer her the clear message that in the midst of life she is close to death. The ghostly-pale funeral director – one of 'actor' Stewart Kirby's eleven roles in von Schnerk's production – provides a haunting image which is both playful and deeply disturbing. It is one of the defining scenes in *Avengers* filmic history.

ZZ von Schnerk, having provided us with a perfect portrait of Emma Peel, sets out the plot for his film in *Avengers* formulaic terms: a "confined, claustrophobic atmosphere" (i.e. interior shots) will be opened out (i.e. location footage) as we witness "Mrs. Peel's descent into the realms of terror." This in turn will lead to the "agonizing climax", "the moment when the heroine is trapped and the diabolical arch-fiend reveals to her his terrifying purpose". Rather than money or world domination, it is to make an "ultimate masterpiece".

Epic, while playing on *The Avengers* formula, is, paradoxically, both reinforcing and undermining it. The episode represents *The Avengers* stripped bare and/or placed in front of a mirror-image of itself. However, it is also unavengerish in its suppression of the realism/surrealism conflict.

When the story leaves the fake/real studio set to take us to Steed – on a real/fake set – we are shown a slate: "Meanwhile...back at the ranch." The suppression of realism continues with Mrs. Peel's refusal to take any of the acting roles seriously, before she playfully roars MGM-lion-style in a superimposed film frame. When Steed arrives to 'save the day' – undermining the mastermind's film script while reinforcing the Avengers' formulaic one – he sits down to read ZZ von Schnerk's script, a story we already know even if we haven't read it.

These surreal, self-referential touches reach a climax with the literal collapse of the 'fourth wall' in the tag scene. Steed kicks down a 'fake' fake wall in Mrs. Peel's apartment on ZZ's studio set within the real Elstree studios. For a viewer, the televisual experience is a baffling, uncomfortable one.

Perhaps one of the most impressive achievements of *Epic* is the fact that despite – or, perhaps, because of – its artificiality – the *studio* studio set creates a genuinely brooding, dark undercurrent. From the moment when Mrs. Peel leaves her replica flat, only to be faced by a host of cameras, there is an atmospheric sense of menace. It is as if the humanised cameras are staring at both her and us. By stripping the show bare, Clemens creates a disturbingly subversive surrealism unlike any other *Avengers* episode.

Brian Clemens has suggested that von Schnerk was based on Erich von Stroheim, of *Sunset Boulevard* fame. Once again, I see this as a half-truth. In the colour era, Clemens often took on the triadic role of writer/script editor/associate producer. ZZ von Schnerk is, in a sense, Brian Clemens, attempting to create the 'ultimate' *Avengers* episode. He had taken control of the series' content by this point and – whether he realised it or not – *Epic* is his celebration of the power he now possessed.

My opinion of *Epic* has dramatically altered over the years. Once upon a time I shared *The Avengers Dossier*'s distaste for its egocentricity. Although I retain certain reservations, I now consider it to be a clever, playfully subversive episode. More importantly, at a historical moment when the series was in danger of becoming stale and predictable, it is ironic that this 'low-cost' mirror-image of *The Avengers* managed to breathe new life into the show.

As a one-off, it is fascinating to watch *The Avengers* and its leading actors revealing and revelling in their own layers of fictionality. The humour is often parody – as when Mrs. Peel tells the actor/policeman that she is "not making a film". It is usually dark, as in the same character's admiration of the extra/corpse's "marvellous breathing control". *Epic* has obvious limitations – and could never have been more than a one-off experiment – but it provided the emerging colour era with a much-needed 'shock of the new'.

Epic (understandably) splits opinion among critics and fans but certainly represents 'subversive champagne'. It is both obviously daring and daringly obvious.

SOMETHING NASTY IN THE NURSERY

Emma: I see a violent death.
Steed: It always starts that way.

A number of Emma Peel-era episodes playfully mock the exclusive, class-bound world of *Avengerland*: the snobbery of a merchant bank, marriage bureau, London hotel, golf club, tie boutique and, perhaps most memorable of all, the SNOB company which trains gentlemen killers. Of course all of these socially exclusive places hide murder beneath a veneer of respectability. *Something Nasty in the Nursery* – with its toy shop for the aristocracy and nanny guild – threatens to add two more organisations or institutions to this sub-genre. However, underneath the humour and satire of this episode, lies something if not nasty then certainly daring, as I seek to explain and explore in this chapter.

The teaser begins with an *Avengers* cliché: an agent running away from an unseen danger. As he enters a private driveway we are provided with the first of a number of teaser twists: the pursuer is an old lady in a motorised wheelchair. The realism of the settings – a suburban road and General Wilmot's study – make way for surrealism as agent Dobson picks up the baby bouncer, its blue and yellow spirals reflecting in his glass lenses. The dramatic chase score is replaced by infantile merry-go-round music as the ball's spinning spirals send us into the victim's hallucination. We are invited to share his 'trip'. Toys and puppets – like dreams – are recurring leitmotifs in *Avengerland* and they always provide a disturbing, dramatic edge. Here a succession of toys leads the way into a child's nursery but Dobson is still an adult, now looking amusingly ridiculous in a large cot. The images on the nursery wallpaper offer us warnings, a form of visual delayed decoding: a Jack of Hearts with a knife in his hand, a man shooting down a bird with his gun, bits of shell exploding out of the muzzle. The stylised, abstract set adds to the odd spectacle. Dobson is now mentally reduced to a small child, his gun representing a water pistol in his innocent little world. When 'nanny' takes his gun and shoots him, his fall in the cot is transformed into him collapsing on the sofa, thumb in mouth as he dies. Even by *Avengers* standards this is a bizarre teaser in which different styles and genres collide. Are we meant to laugh, smile, or treat it as a piece of surreal drama?

The post-teaser scene reverts to *Avengers* clichéd formula: three ministers of the crown are suspected of leaking vital defence secrets. The defence chief describes the allegations as ridiculous: "These men are from the best families; they're British to the core." It is the General's *comment* which is, of course, ridiculous. Strangely, Mrs. Peel backs him up, stating that "these men are above suspicion", without, it would seem, even a hint of irony. In this upper-class world, titles and family heritage provide not only political power but also guaranteed character references. However, as Lord Beaumont becomes the next victim of the hallucinogenic baby bouncer, we witness how simply he reverts to both the language of a private school buffoon – talking about "drinkies" and "goody"– and the behaviour of an infant as he crawls across the rug like a toddler. The instant transformation is far too easy, effortlessly sending these 'responsible men' mentally time-travelling back to a childhood where nanny was god:

"Ball came bouncing in – there I was back in the nursery".

If their titles and 'breeding' place the nobility beyond suspicion what does this tell us about the class-specific apartheid at work in mainstream British culture?

The subsequent scenes in Viscount Webster's house are typical of the unique brand of 'subversive champagne' which only *The Avengers* can offer. The cellar set – more attic than basement – is atmospherically charged: a winding staircase, cobwebs, abandoned furniture, stag's head mounted on the wall, suits of armour behind which an assassin could be lurking. The haunting music helps to create a dramatic tension and we expect the elderly butler to be attacked at any moment. Instead, we see the nanny's blue tights as she pauses outside the cellar window. The inevitable has simply been postponed. On James' return trip to the cellar, his look of terror is all we see, but it is sufficient. It is the perfect example of 'less is more'. As Webster searches for his butler, in the third scene in the cellar, we expect him to uncover the corpse but instead we receive the now-familiar sight of a ball, bouncing down the stairs. We have left the potential murder scene for the absurd vision of the Viscount grinning on a rocking horse. As Emma Peel arrives, the rocking horse has become a rocking chair, Webster sleeping like a baby. It is Mrs. Peel's trip to the cellar which completes the cycle, this time unaccompanied by the musical score, adding to the sense of unease. As a medieval weapon narrowly misses her, a suit of armour collapses, theatrically revealing the dead butler on...a rocking horse. A symbol of playful fun has become one of violence and horror. It is a creepy yet stylish conclusion to this story-within-the-story.

The timeless, tyrannical rules of nobility are reinforced at Martin's toy shop, another wonderful, dazzlingly colourful set in which our eyes feast on train sets, a life-size royal guard and baby bouncers. Even the counter is constructed of giant building blocks. Rather than toys being designed for fun and play, our traditional view of them is undermined again; here they are "created to instil character. Ambition and patriotism." 'Old Martin', at first a seemingly jovial man, is a snob himself, even though he doesn't belong to the exclusive world he serves. He is visibly disappointed that Steed – who we think of as a refined gentleman – is ordinary:

Martin: Just Mister?
Steed: Just.

Martin: Not even an Honourable?
Steed: Afraid not.

In this socially exclusive world, Steed's clothes, accent and manners are not enough to pass muster. He is as much an outsider as we are.

The Guild of Noble Nannies is almost a female equivalent of SNOB in *The Correct Way to Kill*, the gentlemen's marching with bowler and lethal brolly replaced by nannies crisscrossing the training room armed with prams. SNOB's students are, of course, trained killers and here the story plays with and exploits our preconceptions. When the prams converge on him, pinning him against the door, we fear an attack, as does Steed. Umbrella at the ready, he watches the nannies pull out...their rattles, one even winking at him/us. It is a pure moment of subversive champagne. Goat's description of the nannies conforms to traditional gender stereotypes: "sedate, demure, maternal." Steed feels the need to conspire, even dehumanising the nannies as "thoroughbreds of gentility". The scene becomes gently surreal as Steed is left in charge of the 'babies', running around in a futile bid to placate the crying dolls. Odder and odder, as Alice might say.

The familiar triptych structure is completed when Sir George ('Georgie Porgy') receives his baby bouncer, the grin of recognition as he sees it on his car passenger seat confirming that these gentlemen toffs are only too willing to revert to childhood. His baby face as nanny approaches is a wonderfully funny moment, contrasting with the dramatic scene moments later as henchman Gordon attempts to run Emma Peel over. Drama and surreal humour go hand in hand in *Something Nasty in the Nursery*.

As the episode enters its final third, things become more and more bizarre: Steed receives a baby bouncer with a difference – black with 'BOMB' helpfully inscribed on it – and we have entered a comic strip universe. It is also a playfully self-referential one. As Emma Peel suggests Steed pays another visit to Martin's toy shop, the pair openly mock the show's formulaic approach:

Emma: You'd better hurry.
Steed: Why?
Emma: Haven't you noticed – as soon as we discover someone who can supply the answer –
Steed: Someone always gets to them first.

Even Martin's death becomes playful on a number of fronts. First, as Steed enters the shop he finds him lying on the ground. He/we presume that Martin is dead, whereas in fact he is mending a box. Seconds later, on opening another one, he *is* terminated, by a pop-up toy hand brandishing a pistol. Martin almost has time to help Steed to some crucial information but dies in the humorous/melodramatic effort to do so. Can this strange sight be topped? It is, almost immediately, when Gordon and Goat attempt to kill Steed. Initially played straight, as Gordon lies under the Bentley, ready to ambush him, it ends with Steed being attacked by a machine-gun-toting nanny, a visual, surreal highlight of the season.

The short, stylised fight between Emma Peel and Gordon involves Mrs. Peel launching an obligatory pram at him. Three chops later he has been dealt with. After all, there are more important concerns than fight sequences in *Something Nasty in the Nursery*. As Emma picks up a baby bouncer she – pointedly – does not become a grinning, gibbering infant. A split-second flash of childhood toys later she is unconscious. This surely tells us all we need to know about the male victims. Unlike Mrs. Peel, they have never fully grown up; mentally they have one foot still in the nursery.

The amusing finale at the General's home is often criticised by *Avengers* fans and critics. The reason for this is Goat's explanation to Lister about how the Baby Bouncer works – a psychedelic drug absorbed through the skin. This is seen as being heavy-handed. I think this moment has been totally misunderstood by viewers. In this playfully self-referential episode, one which is continually exposing its own fictionality, writer Philip Levene is simply flaunting the *Avengers* formula one last time. It is, in fact, a very clever scene which revolves around what we see and don't see, not the dialogue. At last, nanny is exposed as Goat – which we already knew but wanted to see. More important, dramatically, is the fact that when Steed picks up the ball we don't see that he is wearing gloves, making him immune to the drug-coated Baby Bouncer. The General is more than happy to place the "pretty little missiles" on the map, while we have the delightful spectacle of Steed pretending to be a dog, the missile map firmly wedged between his canines. For the General's sake, the Avengers create a reassuringly childish happy ending: "Once upon a time" (Emma), "there was a big, bad nanny" (Steed). Toffs have to be treated like babies, the message appears to be.

I described the finale as providing us with one final flash of self-referentiality, yet the tag scene adds yet another. More than that, it *is* a piece of self-parody. 'Madame Peel' – hamming it up as far as is humanly possible – reminds us of the *Avengers* formula while gazing into her crystal ball:

Emma: I see a violent death.
Steed: It always starts that way.

Her vision fades just as they enter the "villain's headquarters" where they fight and are "hopelessly trapped". It doesn't matter that the picture clouds over, of course; we know the (never-changing) scenario. She even reminds us to "watch next week". In view of this ending, it seems baffling that so many people have misinterpreted the villains' 'heavy-handed' explanation in the previous scene.

This episode lacks the revolutionary innovation of *Epic* and the darker undercurrents of *Murdersville* but *Something Nasty in the Nursery* is a dazzling, remarkable adventure in the colourful world of *Avengerland*.

THE

JOKER

Strange Young Man: This is a strange situation.
Emma: What do you mean?
Strange Young Man: Tender young woman alone in old dark house. Mysterious stranger calls. "May I use your phone?" She admits him – he picks up the phone…and then…da, da, da, da!…the wires have been cut! The wires *have* been cut. I mean it. Look. Da, da, da, da!

Having seen a mid-season revival in the form of a groundbreaking, self-referential episode, *Epic*, and a quintessentially quirky and colourful *Something Nasty in the Nursery*, *The Avengers* now turned to the past – a video-tape Mrs. Gale episode – to continue Season 5. I suggested in my introduction that the recycling of Cathy Gale material hinted at a lack of new creative ideas. I stick by this judgement, but at the same time it made sound commercial sense – given the increasing time constraints – to return to previously successful episodes rather than turn out a rushed script, as was the case towards the end of Season 4. The Season 3 story *Don't Look Behind You* was tweaked and what emerged was *The Joker*, a stylish remake, arguably far more atmospheric than the original.

Given that a key ingredient in *The Avengers'* recipe for success is the Steed/Peel, Macnee/Rigg rapport, it is ironic that three of the season's most satisfying episodes are (virtual) 'one-handers'. As with much of the series' history, there is serendipity at work here. These episodes provided either one or the other of the lead actors with some much-needed rest from a gruelling rehearsal/shooting schedule. When Steed falls down his staircase – thanks to Max Prendergast's trip wire – we are being warned that *The Joker* will be a Steed 'holiday episode'. This is confirmed by Mrs. Peel's warning: "You'll have to stay off that leg for a while".

The Joker continues the Steed/Peel running gag of Emma Peel's ever-expanding repertoire of mental and physical expertise. This started in the very first episode, *The Town of No Return*, with her fencing. As I suggested in my analysis of the monochrome season, it both reinforces yet playfully undermines our image of her as an intellectually and physically brilliant, emancipated female. Here, Steed confesses that he found her article about Bridge baffling:

"All bids, no trumps and mathematics. It was very confusing."

Mrs. Peel's exhilaratingly independent image is reinforced as the film cuts between the laid-up, convalescing Steed and Emma speeding along in her Lotus on a carefree, country drive.

The gender dynamics in *The Joker* are interesting. Max Prendergast – a mass killer of refugees who Mrs. Peel once tricked into being arrested in Berlin – is seen as a disturbed, damaged, male voyeur. Having lured her to a remote, unoccupied mansion, he continually spies on Emma in her bedroom, through a peep hole. His (mostly) invisible presence is played chillingly straight, unlike that of the hired – then executed – 'strange young man'. The latter is at once ridiculous – arriving in sunglasses despite the blanket of fog – yet also playfully menacing. He attempts to exert his physical strength and sexual 'charm' on Mrs. Peel. This has a paradoxical effect on both Emma and the viewer. It reinforces the brooding, darkly dramatic undercurrent, but also creates humour. When he accuses her of cutting the telephone wires in order to keep him at Sir Cavalier's mansion, she verbally puts him down:

Strange Young Man: *You* – you did it to keep me here.
Emma: Now why would I want to do that?
Strange Young Man: I've got vitality, charm.
Emma: You've got a vivid imagination.

She then physically overpowers him, despite his knife, throwing him out of the house. He is pushed back through the front entrance, like a disgraced, hormonal teenager who has overstepped the perimeter of acceptable social/sexual behaviour.

Ola's positioning in these gender dynamics is more complex. Professing to be a budding actress, her role seems to be that of a disturbed, sadistic woman who thinks she is sane but is 'playing' at being strange. As with the young man, our initial response is to dismiss Ola as a ridiculous over-the-top figure. This is reinforced as she hams up the cliché of the creepy, gothic atmosphere:

"I love the dark...owl time. Full of all sorts of creeps and crawls and chill spines. All sorts of tingles."

Our dismissal of her as harmlessly freakish is slowly undermined, reaching a climax with the disturbing image of her manically cutting the fish. Like Emma Peel, we are unsure now as to how we should 'read' her. Is she insanely playful, or playfully insane?

Our growing sense of double or even triple bluff can be extended to the story as a whole. *The Joker* uses the established house of horror genre and, by undermining it, manages to heighten the sense of fear. All the *Hammer* ingredients are there: the isolated house at "the end of the world"; the young, attractive female 'victim'; the impenetrable curtain of fog; suits of armour and tall, dark furniture, ideal for hiding behind. This is then teasingly added to by Ola's "dreamy" language and the unexpected arrival of the 'mysterious stranger':

Strange Young Man: This is a strange situation.
Emma: What do you mean?
Strange Young Man: Tender young woman alone in old dark house. Mysterious stranger calls. "May I use your phone?" She admits him – he picks up the phone...and then...da, da, da, da!...the wires have been cut! The wires *have* been cut. I mean it. Look. Da, da, da, da!

He sends up the cliché of their "movie situation" – his original phrase which was cut – before re-establishing it. His final "da, da, da, da!" leaves us unsure – once again – how to react. It is a moment of pure subversive champagne.

The joker/death staircase door is both mildly ridiculous yet disconcerting. Its artificiality – as so often in *The Avengers* –

heightens the disturbing atmosphere. This also applies to the enormous playing card faces in the dining room. Described by Ola as "very friendly", these cardboard cut-outs take on an irrationally threatening feel. While writer Brian Clemens had in mind that their faces would "seem almost human, their eyes staring at Emma Peel", it is, I feel, the distinct possibility of someone hiding behind them – as with the corridor furniture – which creates the underlying tension.

The writer and director allow us to see more than Mrs. Peel: the man standing statue-still in the grounds while Ola mentions "murderer"; the movement under the dust sheet in the rocking chair room; the eye at the peep-hole. Nevertheless, the camera often asks us to share Emma's fear. This is particularly effective when Prendergast's mind games reach their crescendo. The camera whips round the hall and staircase, sometimes offering us her viewpoint, while the diabolical mastermind provides a mocking commentary:

"I might be here you see. Or I might be right behind you. Do you see me? Am I close enough to stretch out my hand and touch you? The key has gone, Emma. You won't get out that way."

It is at this precise moment – perhaps even more than in Season 6's wonderfully chilling *Take-Over* – when *The Avengers* comes as close as it ever does to creating pure fear, with Prendergast's assertion that he doesn't want to frighten her/us darkly ironic, simply thickening the dramatic moment.

Steed's arrival – knocking Prendergast out with one of the giant cards – fails to lift the mood. For once we have experienced a surfeit of fear. His reassurance – "it's morning now, the fog's lifted. Let's get a breath of fresh air" – embraces the viewer as well as Mrs. Peel.

The Joker is an unsettling, subversive episode in which our clichéd, irrational fears are played with, as we are forced to share Prendergast's "mad, warped sense of humour". It is also an opportunity for Diana Rigg to display a wider range of her acting ability and talent, which is not always the case in this colour season. It is, frequently, the episodes which revolve around mind games which are the most memorable, testing actors and audience to the limit.

WHO'S WHO???

Emma: Steed, that woman, it's not me.
Steed: Save your breath, Mrs. Peel. That's not me either.

Who's Who??? belongs to a sub-genre of *Avengers* filmed episodes which plays on the idea of doppelgangers or doubles. This includes *Two's A Crowd, They Keep Killing Steed* and *The New Avengers* episode *Faces*. They allow the series to experiment, with the actors leaving their comfort zone by taking on alternative roles; they also test the viewer's ability to reach beyond the obvious fact that it is the real actors taking on secondary roles.

Who's Who??? begins with a stylishly bizarre and self-referential teaser. We open with a close-up of a rose, warning us that this will be a significant object. It is being worn by Hooper, an agent, who enters a warehouse full of crates. The realism of the set is at odds with his attire. He is wearing a Steed-like bowler and carrying an umbrella. Already we have been introduced to the theme of doubles before the plot has even kicked off. The large crates provide an unsettling backdrop, perfect places for a villain to hide behind. The seemingly deserted nature of the set/location adds to the atmosphere. We watch him moving around from above and then through a distorting glass, suggesting that we can expect an episode in which we will have to view events from alternative angles. Basil and Lola pop up out of two of the crates – like malevolent jack-in-the-boxes – and shoot him. They place one of the guns on the ground, with the rose stem in the nozzle as if in a vase. It is like a piece of postmodern art, or a publicity still for *The Avengers* itself. It also self-referentially echoes the first image in the opening titles sequence.

Just as we expect the teaser to end, the camera pans out to reveal a far more bizarre image: the gun is framed by an enormous pair of trouser legs – on stilts, in fact – above which Hooper's corpse is perched on a lofty crate, like a grotesque version of Steed himself, on display. Our thoughts echo Emma's at the beginning of the post-teaser scene: "Now I have seen everything", Steed's dark humoured response – "he's a very upright fellow" – warning us that any disturbing undercurrent will be kept playfully at bay in this episode.

The self-referential nature of *Who's Who???* is confirmed by the scene in which Basil and Lola watch a film of Emma Peel and John Steed. Their respective comments about our heroes being "delectable, ravishing" and "poised, charming" add both humour and an early sense of conflict as jealousy rears its ugly head. Later, Lola criticises Basil for 'slouching' "like a peasant" while Steed "has poise, a touch of the aristocrat".

Dr. Krelmar's brain-swapping machine is obviously ridiculous but part of the fun of the episode lies in the way that the characters' mannerisms are transferred to their new bodies: Lola's chewing gum and Basil's habit of playing with dice, biting cigars and suffering from migraines. There is also an intertwined second layer of wit as the uncouth villains struggle to mirror the suave and sophisticated Steed and Mrs. Peel. In a sense, this is a comedy of manners, offering us the warning that you might be able to swap clothes, voices and bodies, but *The Avengers*' class-bound world cannot be stormed by brutal masterminds. Conversely, it also pokes fun at that elitist world, one in which the Major states that "I know an old Etonian when I meet one...that chap in there's [Steed] no gentleman."

The viewer's experience is always a strange, amusingly unsettling one in this sub-genre of episode. While Mrs. Peel is still Mrs. Peel but Basil has become Steed we can enjoy Basil's discomfort as he is asked to help himself to a drink: "You know where it is" and slips up by calling her "Emma". On the other hand, our experience is transformed and scrambled – subverted even – when Mrs. Peel has also been replaced. Suddenly we have the weirdly surreal sight of Patrick Macnee and Diana Rigg playing an amorous, uncouth couple, out of their (fictional) characters yet still in their own bodies. It adds an extra fictional level to the spectacle, as Macnee plays Basil playing Steed. It also tests our ability to cope with the warped vision as, for example Basil (now 'Steed') complains that it hurt him when Lola smacked Steed ('Basil'):

Emma: Steed, that woman, it's not me.
Steed: Save your breath, Mrs. Peel. That's not me either.

As if to emphasise the artfully artificial nature of the script and to revel in our potential confusion, we then see an 'important announcement' card on screen, a 'real' voice intruding into the episode:

"For the benefit of those who have only just switched on to *The Avengers*, we'd like to explain that these two villains [photo of Basil and Lola] have swapped minds with Steed and Emma. So at the moment the villains look like this [photo of the Avengers] while Steed and Emma look like this [photo of Basil and Lola]. Got it? This is Steed [Basil] and this is Emma [Lola] and these are the villains [photo of the Avengers]. At least I think they are. On with the show."

The playfully patronising 'public information' announcement is clearly not designed to be informative, but rather to disrupt any lingering sense of realism and add another layer of self-referentiality to the surreal, colourful world of Season 5.

The humour of the episode threatens to descend into unsubtle slapstick as the villains visit the Major's office, the wall and ceiling decorated with an enormous Union Jack, the work surfaces covered with tall thin vases representing the 'floral network'. Agent Tulip even describes himself as "blooming" and Basil and Lola continue to bump off the Major's "bouquet of agents", starting with Daffodil and Poppy. As the related metaphors go into hyper-drive, in Steed's own words the 'floral network' is in danger of becoming a "barren garden". From some respects, the Major's description of the heroes'/villains' "ridiculous charade" could refer to our own viewing experience.

A second "very important announcement" warns us that while the spectacle and storyline are "very confusing", "it will all sort itself out". There is a paradox at play here. The announcements threaten to disrupt the *Avengers* formula, only to reassure us that there will be a comforting, formulaic ending.

Who's Who??? is, ultimately, an episode which pokes fun at its own fictional world, one in which Steed is more upset about the last of his 1947 champagne being drunk unchilled and his cigar ends bitten off than the fact that his very identity has been stolen:

Steed: What sort of a fiend are we dealing with? A man who would bite the end off a cigar is capable of anything!

Despite Basil and Lola's decision to remain in "permanent residence" as Steed and Mrs. Peel – leading to the official order to kill the real Avengers – there is no darker edge to *Who's Who?* It lacks the dramatic subversion of many of the other episodes, even though it remains a clever, highly entertaining comedy of manners. There is plenty of 'champagne' but the subversion is purely visual, as the game of doubles is amusingly played out:

Lola ('Emma'): Steed and Mrs. Peel seem to be just good friends.
Basil ('Steed'): Well if they were, they'll be a lot friendlier from now on.

The script could have been developed into a disturbing *Avengers* 'hour', with tension rising as the cupboard of corpses in the apartment fills and Emma Peel and Steed search for the machine before it is destroyed and/or they are eliminated by their own side. Instead, we have a witty, thoroughly enjoyable but less challenging experience which reflects the general evolution of the Emma Peel era.

DEATH'S DOOR

Emma: You know my wave length.
Steed: I do indeed.

Epic and *Murdersville* are radical, disruptive films which demonstrate that, even at this (relatively) late point in *The Avengers*' history, the series was still capable of reinventing itself. *Death's Door* is not a radical episode. What it does represent, though, is one of the best examples of what *The Avengers* 'in colour' should have been doing all along. It has one foot in the well-made Season 4 vintage and one in the more psychedelic, colourful world of the new.

The 'cocktail recipe' might read as follows: take the tried and tested *Avengers* ingredient of a decent plot, well researched and hovering on the borderline between realism/surrealism; whisk in some witty dialogue; add some visually striking leitmotifs and imagery; mix in a memorable mastermind; decorate with interesting locations and sets; add some experimental camera angles. Shake thoroughly. Serves a thirsty, faithful public.

Death's Door has a simple, well-made plot. Delegates are meeting in London to form a ground-breaking United Europe. The Eastern Bloc mastermind has anaesthetic darts fired into the presiding delegate, who is then taken to a 'set' where a manufactured reality is played out under drugged/dream conditions. The end resembles a premonition of death. As soon as the 'dream' details are repeated in the president's daytime he is too petrified to pass through the conference room's 'death door'. As Steed tries to convince Lord Melford:

"Your nightmare was a reality. But they made you believe it was a dream…Then it was enough to make a dream come true."

The 'dream' sequences are atmospherically shot and allow the writer/director to undermine certain polarities such as: sleep/awake. The traditional divide is blurred and sleep becomes both disturbed and disturbing. Oneiric sequences are nearly always well done in *The Avengers*. Here, the subsequent 'real' experiences – fulfilling the 'dream' premonitions – are equally atmospheric and...dream-like.

Some of the props used by the mastermind to create the illusion are standard *Avengers* fare, such as the giant calendar which would reappear in *Mission...Highly Improbable*. Others, particularly the featureless faces of the bowler-clad businessmen, are disturbingly surreal.

The scenes which take place at Becker's warehouse – "Nightmare Alley" as Mrs. Peel names it – are part of *The Avengers*' continuing interest in self-referentiality and metafiction: another of those sets-within-sets. What are we meant to make of Mrs. Peel's comment to Lord Melford?

"Everything you see here are props. Just props."

The warehouse sequences, on one level, provide Melford/us with a tour of an avengerish *Avengers* set.

As with many of the well-made *Avengers* scripts, there is a beautifully playful symmetry to the structure: two terrified presiding delegates making two real/nightmarish journeys; two failures to cross the death's door threshold; Steed and Mrs. Peel are then involved in parallel fight scenes, Steed's on Becker's target range, Mrs. Peel's with the chauffeur in Steed's flat. Steed's is particularly memorable as he/the camera/we look through the target board bullet hole at Becker, advancing towards us with his rifle. Both scenes end with the Avenger discovering a key to the 'dream warehouse' on the body of the defeated enemy. While both scenes are played 'straight', the mirror-image endings are humorously neat and aesthetically pleasing, yet do not undermine the dramatic tension.

The Steed/Peel dynamics are central to the episode's success. When Steed passes Emma a walkie-talkie, and confirms that he knows her wave length, there are not only the literal and sexual meanings at play, but a more general sense of a wonderfully warm rapport.

Both Avengers are deeply cynical about politicians and their entourages. Frank Stapley, the press attaché (and diabolical mastermind) is wonderfully sent-up. On reading his cover-up newspaper article, Mrs. Peel admires his "double talk":

Emma: Why Sir Andrew left the conference or how to say nothing in five hundred well-chosen words.
Steed: Stapley can't help telling half-truths. He's in constant touch with politicians.

The witty dialogue almost has the feel of a Season 4 episode. Even the straight-laced Lord Melford and Stapley get in on the act:

Melford: You're a first rate liar, Stapley.
Stapley: Thank you, sir.

The featureless faces of the bureaucrats from Lord Melford's manufactured dreams are not only disturbingly surreal. On another level they gently poke fun at the faceless bureaucracy, half-truths and lies created and then distributed by the political world. This seems to be a timeless critique!

Death's Door is not perfect. The final, speeded-up fight sequence is poorly done and 'pacifist' Stapley's reasoning for the sabotage is never explained. However, if *Something Nasty in the Nursery* is the ideal episode to show a newcomer to Season 5 in terms of the new, wacky *Avengerland* then *Death's Door* is arguably the best in terms of the 'even' evolution from monochrome to colour which sometimes emerged. This is how it could and possibly should have been done, but rarely was.

YOU HAVE JUST BEEN MURDERED

Needle: You have just been murdered again...For the fourth time... Four times is the limit, Mr. Rathbone. The next time, it'll be for real.

You Have Just Been Murdered is a paradox: it is both familiarly formulaic yet also deliciously inventive. A series of important men being frightened and/or blackmailed is a familiar Philip Levene Season 5 scenario, connecting to other episodes such as *The Fear Merchants* and *Death's Door*. However, the memorable, dastardly mastermind, Nathaniel Needle, his surreal *Avengerland* haystack headquarters and the stylish henchman with his calling cards combine to offer us a magical, polished 'hour'.

The teaser sets the tone, style and thematic content for the entire episode. As businessman Gilbert Jarvis arrives at his country house the music warns us that someone is already there, lurking in the shadows. A smouldering cigarette butt in the cut-glass ashtray tells Jarvis what we already sense, that he has unwelcome company. As we see a gloved hand lock the door, we are once again ahead of him; he has simply heard the sound. *Avengers* clichés are being introduced only to then be undermined. The obligatory search for the desk drawer pistol reveals that the henchman, Skelton, already has it, while our assumption that Jarvis will be terminated is also played with: the pistol is fore-grounded as it is aimed at him, the barrel seen turning as beads of sweat appear on his face. As it clicks we/he discover that it isn't loaded. The businessman – like us as viewers – has been teased. As the wonderful scene comes to a close, Skelton, now standing by the curtained French windows, flicks his calling card onto the study desk: "You have just been murdered". A business card from a hit-man warning his potential victim-client that he *means* business: pure *Avengers*.

However bizarre the card's warning appears to be, we can already make an educated guess as to the mastermind's theatrical plan. Maybe we can even anticipate the black humour which will arise, as victims warn the Avengers that they have been 'murdered'. What we don't expect is the teasingly drawn-out nature of the intimidation, as further cards/warnings follow: "You have just been murdered – again!" The extended gag works in terms of gallows humour. It seems less funny when it becomes "you are *about* to be murdered" and the game has been transformed into a deadly serious one, cranking up the dramatic undercurrent. Skelton is the latest in an effective line of assassin henchmen: chillingly handsome, well-dressed, urbane, smiling and – most importantly – deadly silent.

Levene's script offers a critique of the capitalist 'community' of businessmen millionaires. In the post-teaser scene, Steed describes George Unwin's parties:

"Three main topics of conversation. Money, how to make it, how to hold on to it. Very dull, unless one's income is in the seven figure bracket."

Steed is not displaying envy here. Neither he nor Emma Peel suffers from the green-eyed monster, jealousy. With luxurious apartments, fashionable clothes, expensive cars and glamorous looks why would they? Their world of excitement, vitality, adventure and danger is a polarised opposite of that of the moneyed, staid guests we encounter at Unwin's party. Despite the presence of glamorous waitresses wearing top hats and revealing tails, the men mostly look bored or fearful. Steed describes the *ambience*: "that heady aroma...the sweet, sickly smell of money". Rathbone, who Mrs. Peel spies at the party, will be the next victim although herein lies a (minor) problem with the script. A millionaire who is so miserably 'tight' that he even steals cigarettes at a party he has been invited to cannot gain our sympathy. Indeed, we almost enjoy seeing him squirm. The fact that these millionaires are living in fear behind locks, bolts and guard dogs isn't enough to makes us care, not when their characters are as unpleasantly dull as Rathbone's is.

Mrs. Peel's schoolteacherly treatment of the diminutive Rathbone at his house offers a welcome moment of humour and wit, as she chastises him for his party 'theft':

Rathbone: You used a dishonest trick to -
Emma: And you know all about dishonesty don't you Mr. Rathbone.
Rathbone: Well, they were there to take.
Emma: But not to take away. Naughty!

The amusing confrontation also makes us wonder about the honesty of these millionaires. What other unwritten rules have they broken in order to become filthy rich? Their subsequent conversation includes an ideological debate about 'thriftiness', Rathbone arguing that it "breeds moral character" – his actions have already disproved that theory – while Emma suggests that it gathers "dust". It isn't money itself which is seen as the problem, but what people do with it. In our Avengers' world it is to be spent sexily: sports cars, fashionable clothes and champagne; not to gather dust in mothballed, dull mansions. We can be fairly sure that Rathbone lived in this rich man's prison – protected by high walls, guards and security locks – even before the blackmail began. Is this the price he pays for being wealthy? Is it worth it? His frightened little face which peers out at Chalmers from behind the chain-locked door provides us with the answer. Mrs. Peel describes Rathbone's home as "a fortress. Guards, barred windows..." Part of the dark humour arises from the fact that rich men are hiding away in these padlocked 'cells' but nothing they put in place can prevent Needle from striking:

Needle: You have just been murdered again...For the fourth time... Four times is the limit, Mr. Rathbone. The next time, it'll be for real.

By the time George Unwin becomes the latest victim the dramatic effect has been lost on us – though not him – as we now know that no one is murdered first time out. We are able to sit back and simply enjoy the surreal spectacle. Levene will later startle us, though, when Unwin is shot with an arrow, the rubber end leaving a neat 'you have just been murdered' print on his shirt. These clever touches and variations add to the style of the episode, surprising us at the very moment when we think we have fully understood the formulaic pattern.

Talk of enjoying the spectacle brings me to Needle himself, played with consummate ease and style by George Murcell. There are not many better masterminds in either Emma Peel season. He has a wonderfully dry sense of humour and is clearly relishing every minute of his master plan. His use of the television to communicate with Unwin is a particularly effective, self-referential touch. His enjoyment even rubs off on us and it is hard to completely dislike him:

"The name is Needle. No quips please. I've heard them all before. Although I do admit that I am a little difficult to find. Extremely unwise to try. Now someone once said that a man should use his natural born talents to the full...I'm a natural born parasite."

Even when threatened by potential danger, he manages a clever retort:

Nicholls: Rathbone was followed. Some woman, tall, slim, auburn haired –
Needle: Never mind her attributes, deal with her quickly.

When henchman Skelton finally speaks it is clear that he shares his boss' line in dry wit:

Needle: Did you manage to pin Mr. Unwin down?
Skelton: Well he was in more of an upright position when I pinned him against a wall. I damaged his orchid.

The repartee and sense of humour which they share offers an interesting, demonic mirror image of Steed and Emma Peel's delightful banter.

Emma Peel's fight with Nicholls recalls previous eras as she is wearing a leather cat-suit for the only time in colour and the location – Tykes Water Lake bridge – is the iconic setting for so many memorable monochrome scenes. The fight is an example of 'subversive champagne', combining the humour of Emma's stick being slowly whittled away and the gruesome conclusion as the henchman lands on his own scythe. Later, she fights another 'heavy' (a frogman) in the lake itself, before ordering him to take her "to your leader". Once again, Levene's story surprises us as we discover that Unwin's million has a bomb attached to it, thus providing us with a potentially explosive finale. As we reach the climax, even businessman Unwin (unwittingly?) gets in on the witty dialogue:

Unwin: Look Steed, I'm sorry. I should have told you – but I *have* been murdered four times.
Steed: If anything happens to Mrs. Peel there'll be a fifth.

Needle's haystack headquarters is a perfect one for such a practical joker. It also adds a distinctly surreal touch to the closing minutes of *You Have Just Been Murdered*. Even more bizarre is the sight of Needle – post bomb – blasted into a tree and still clutching the steering wheel of his Land Rover in death. That is about as odd an image as we see in the Emma Peel era, or any other. No wonder Steed and Emma's reaction is to stare at the tree with a bemused look, before gently laughing.

In general, *You Have Just Been Murdered* follows a familiar *Avengers* pattern and structure, but it is an episode with so many clever touches, a wonderful mastermind and an ingenuously simple premise that it stands out from similarly formulaic Season 5 films, enchanting us with its unusual wit and charm.

MURDERSVILLE

Forbes: I must say, this *is* a friendly little place.

It seems appropriate that my journey through the *Avengerland* of the Emma Peel era – which began with *The Town of No Return* – should end with *Murdersville*. In many ways these two episodes are companion pieces. *Murdersville* is more style-conscious – the colour focusing or forcing our attention on Mrs. Peel's (purple) jumpsuit and her elegant (egg-shell metallic blue) Lotus – and the budget is clearly far bigger, emphasised by the (unavengerish) helicopter chase. However, beneath the cosmetic differences, the two episodes have a great deal in common: 'idyllic' villages where the welcome is distinctly frosty and where, in the words of imprisoned vicar James Purser:

"Anything can happen…Anything at all."

Little Bazeley by-the-sea and Little Storping in-the-Snuff have dangerously unfriendly pubs which illustrate precisely this. The Inebriated Gremlin and The Happy Ploughman are the starting-points for deadly pursuits: human 'badger hunting' or pre-paid assassinations. *Murdersville*'s Mickle is an even more disturbing henchman than Saul, revelling in the violence and happily fantasising about what he will do to Mrs. Peel before she joins the growing list of corpses.

Murdersville is the penultimate film in the Peel era. Its 'teaser' illustrates the close connections between it and Clemens' opening monochrome film, two episodes which almost represent book-ends of the Peel era:

Mickle: Nice day, Hubert.
Hubert: Ah. It *is* a nice day.
Mickle: Yesterday was nice too.
Hubert: Ah. Yesterday *was* a nice day. Might rain, though.
Mickle: Oh, I dunno. [Assassination takes place in front of them]. You might be right, Hubert – a funny old day. Might rain.

The dialogue is banal in the best Pinteresque tradition. The conversation between the two village locals is as absurdly at odds with what we see – the murder which takes place beside their dominoes board – as was that between Saul and the fake Brandon as the latter emerged from the sea impeccably dressed in a (dry) tweed jacket and tie. Brandon's parting comment – "looks like rain" – is echoed here by the friends' agreement that it "might rain". As I suggested in that opening chapter, on one level this represents pathetic fallacy: beneath the sunny, chocolate-box-cottage veneer, Little Storping is (metaphorically-speaking) a dark place. It also offers us an immediate warning that nothing can be taken at face value. Our thoughts at this moment match Emma Peel's later comment: "I don't know what's happening here".

Both these teasers remind me of Harold Pinter's comment that "underneath what is being said, something else is being said". He was referring to his own plays' playfully mundane dialogue but it applies equally well to the subversively surreal suppression of realism in *The Avengers*.

Humour in *Murdersville* takes a disconcerting number of forms. Major Croft's faithful retainer, Forbes, is blissfully unaware of the village's deadly secret. This gives rise to a darkly ironic humour. As Mickle and Hubert delay him in the pub, he happily sups his 'free' pint: "I must say, this *is* a friendly little place." His praise is delivered just as the landlord passes a gun to a killer in conspicuous sunglasses. Shortly afterwards, this is echoed by Forbes' gratitude as the locals arrive while he is unloading the Major's belongings. Anticipating their assistance, he positively sings his praise: "That's what I call neighbourly". Their destruction of all the valuables seconds later literally shatters his naïve belief in rural conviviality.

The scene is a deeply unpleasant one, yet sometimes the dark humour manages, paradoxically, to be light-hearted. When an assassin enters Little Storping's library, he is reminded by the strict librarian of the 'Silence' sign hanging up. He attaches a ridiculously-sized silencer to his pistol before terminating his victim. The library's customers happily continue their activities. This is, after all, *Avengerland*, where anything can happen and nothing is what it seems.

The obligatory fight ending – involving cream cakes – is part of *Murdersville*'s slapstick comedy. It is arguably the most cleverly and humorously choreographed fight in the series. This 'froth' begins with the first museum scene. The light tone of the music, as the camera pans around an assortment of historical torture equipment – an Iron Maiden, seat of nails, prisoner's iron cage etc. – reassures us that this will not be one of the episode's many darker scenes, even before we see Mrs. Peel locked in a chastity belt. The light-hearted, surreal comedy is increased as she is informed that the gagged woman – in a scold's cradle – is the ex-telephone operator who is being punished because the villagers "thought she was yelling too much."

Watching *Murdersville* is a disconcerting experience. This is partly explained by the way the humour veers between cruel, dark irony and the aforementioned slapstick. It is also because, whenever the 'froth' is lifted, we are confronted by a chilling story. At one point Dr. Haymes warns Emma Peel: "You are going to disappear. You were never in Little Storping." Her heartfelt reply – "I wish that were true" – is (almost) shared by us at the moments when the disturbing realism and/or surrealism dominate.

The village pond ducking scene becomes increasingly unsettling, as does the one where Mrs. Peel is surrounded by the entire village before the helicopter chase. However, it is the scene in Dr. Haymes' surgery which is the most upsetting. Mrs. Peel's discovery of her lifelong friend's corpse offers us a rare moment of real pathos in the series. In the makeshift morgue, the camera zooms in on Paul Croft's dead face and Emma's own expresses a tearful, raw emotion. Her sorrow and anger bring her to within a split-second of dashing Haymes' brains out with the telephone. The genuine emotion is, arguably, unavengerish, but is deeply touching.

Talk of unavengerish brings me on to the helicopter chase. Despite – or perhaps because of – the season's earlier problems with finance, I see the decision to use one here as an unnecessary revelling in the flashier, glamorous colour *Avengerland*. The scene is far too long and – rather like the anti-hunt demonstrators in *Silent Dust* or the special effects in many of the Season 5/6 episodes – seems out of place in *The Avengers*. It is a faintly absurd scene but this absurdity may have been part of Clemens' thinking. After all, we have been warned that anything can happen in both Little Storping and the colourful *Avengers*.

The late arrival of Steed – in another of his holiday episodes – brings welcome relief not only for Mrs. Peel but also for the viewer in the form of witty dialogue, something which the episode had previously lacked. It is (comically) inevitable that he would be required to unlock Mrs. Peel from the chastity belt:

"It may surprise you to know that I've had very little experience with this type of garment."

His summing up of the unfriendly local pub is equally sharp:

"The landlord was extremely inhospitable. He came at me with a twelve bore…I didn't even criticise the beer."

In a priceless moment, as the henchmen arrive for the final attack, Steed warns the gagged Hilary: "Not a word."

Murdersville is, like *The Town of No Return*, an iconic *Avengers* episode. It takes us on a rollercoaster of emotions to an unprecedented extent in the series' history. It demonstrates that *The Avengers*, even at the end of Season 5, still retained the spirit of the show so apparent at the beginning of the (monochrome) filmed era. *Murdersville* also suggests that, even if the plots/stories were becoming simplified, there were, conversely, more artistic risks being taken. Some of these didn't work, but others — such as *Murdersville*'s daring interplay between a savage realism and a subversive surrealism — do come off, with spectacular results.

The Avengers had endured an 'uneven' evolution in colour. The genuinely innovative episodes were in a minority, with not enough 'individual' films testing the formulaic *Avengers* structure. However, at its best — as it is here — the colour Peel season demonstrates its ability to be revolutionary in the viewing experience it offered its audience.

Murdersville is, in the words of its writer, "very, very sinister" yet offering an "amusing" experience. This might sound like a highly improbable mission but here we have the proof that the subversive champagne could still flow as the series reached the end of its penultimate season.

CONCLUSION

At the heart of *The Avengers* is a series of terminal paradoxes. It was a show which often reinforced contemporary sexist traits and trends, yet which played a key, countercultural role in the gender politics of the era. It engaged with serious social concerns – such as the Cold War, espionage, nuclear weapons, advancing technology, the potential dangers of scientific experimentation, mind-orientation drugs, consumerism and capitalism – but refused to take them or itself (too) seriously. It has frequently been described as 'timeless' – and has certainly not dated to the same extent as many of its contemporaries – yet was clearly context-dependent, a product of the ever-changing cultural politics of the 1960s. It is revered for its distinct celebration of a class-bound Englishness yet its continuation – in its colour filmed era – relied solely on American investment. One of its key ingredients is the rapport between the male/female lead actors/characters, yet some of the most satisfying episodes are (virtual) 'one-handers': *Epic*, *The Joker*, *Murdersville*, *Stay Tuned* and *Take-Over*. Paradox is at its core and is part of its appeal, charm, complexity and continuing ability to thrill viewers.

The majority of *Avengers* fans and critics agree that the monochrome, filmed Season 4 represents the pinnacle of the show's artistic achievement. As I suggested in my introduction, it is a major turning-point, caught at the crossroads between studio-bound video tape and 'glorious Technicolor'. Season 4 had the fortune of being able to provide a televisual quality unavailable in the video-taped era. It also avoided some – though by no means all – of the cartoonish excesses which (adversely) affected many of the later colour episodes. I remain convinced that the financial necessity to film in black and white enhanced the look of the season, offering a 'classy' purity and clarity lacking in the following seasons. Jaz Wiseman and Robert Banks Stewart discuss this on the DVD commentary of *The Master Minds*:

RBS: Colour makes you more 'showbusy entertainy'. Black and white *invested*.
JW: There's a real depth in terms of the quality, the contrast, and the lighting has to be great…The black and white Emma Peel is the peak of the show.
RBS: If you are going to film in colour you want to be 'colourful' and you're maybe sometimes drawn into filming locations for location sake.
JW: This retains a certain *noir* quality in terms of the directing and the acting. There are shots where it's very black and then suddenly you get a face coming out. The black and white adds to the storylines and plot. And the enjoyment.
RBS: It adds to the *menace*.

It is a fascinating conversation and it is clear that both Wiseman and Banks Stewart agree that the monochrome film season is able to create an atmosphere which is lost in colour. Banks Stewart suggests that colour can distract, drawing writer and director away from what really matters. This is, I feel, the case with *The Avengers*. This remains a subjective, unquantifiable viewpoint, of course. However, even Brian Clemens – desperate for *The Avengers* to go into colour as soon as it went on to film – has since admitted that monochrome looks "more real than colour". The 'look' was key by Season 4, with post-production editing deemed as important as the writing and directing.

My selection of episodes – from both of the filmed Emma Peel seasons – will, naturally, be more controversial. Every viewer/critic has his/her personal favourites. The fact that many of my monochrome choices come from early on in Season 4 reflects my belief that it was *during* that period that the show began to lose its way in terms of artistic quality and thematic balance. Despite this, there are some excellent episodes in the 'uneven' era of Season 5 (and even more in the following Tara King season), and I hope that my exploration of *Epic, Something Nasty in the Nursery, The Joker, Death's Door, You Have Just Been Murdered* and *Murdersville* demonstrates that – at its best – *The Avengers* 'in colour' produced episodes which were as good as anything in the entire run. *Epic* and *Murdersville*, in particular, are startlingly radical, disruptive visual texts which demonstrate that the series was still capable of reinventing itself when it took genuine artistic risks.

Some of the late-season episodes in Season 4 have a 'rushed' feel in terms of the plot structure. This is understandable given that the production time constraints sometimes required Brian Clemens – who decided to write most of these final episodes – or another writer to turn a script around within a couple of days. Some of these late-season episodes also, arguably, over-do the English eccentricity of *The Avengers*, possibly with an American market in mind. This was to become a common failing in the last two seasons; at the same time, as David K Smith reminds us, it was thanks to the Americans – who were funding the show by this point – that we still had an *Avengers* series to enjoy.

Not every episode provides us with 'subversive champagne'. For me, the groundbreaking ones are those which offer a 'constant interplay' between realism and surrealism; light entertainment but with dark, dramatic edges. It is these episodes which offer the viewer disruptive borderline fictions which reach beyond traditional genres. At its best, *The Avengers* requires its television viewers to be active participants rather than passive consumers. Despite the comforting closure of the 'tag' scenes, it asks questions which stay with us after our heroes have happily exited towards the 'bright horizon' (in monochrome) or brought the episode to an amusing, frothy close (in colour).

Avengerland is a state of mind rather than a geographical location. Airbases, coastal villages, department stores, warehouses, miniature railways, Christmas displays, country mansions, childhood nurseries, cottage hospitals, cat sanctuaries and specialist shops are all, in theory, banal and ordinary. However, given a well-balanced interplay of genres and styles they can become extraordinary places in which almost anything is possible. This is a series which even made a real *studio* studio set chilling and disturbing.

I have explored *The Avengers*' use of self-referentiality on a number of occasions in this study. This, in itself, does not make the specific episode or the series subversive or innovative. It is the fact that the writers are playfully exposing the drama's fictionality while maintaining – or even heightening – our dramatic interest which makes it interesting. It is often when *The Avengers* is at its most playfully artificial that the darker undercurrents are most effective. More paradoxes!

There is plenty of variety in both seasons. This is particularly true in Season 4 where claustrophobic, studio-based dramas such as *The Murder Market*, *Dial A Deadly Number* and *Death at Bargain Prices* are balanced out by the agoraphobic, location-based freedom of *Silent Dust* and *The Hour That Never Was*.

One or two of the episodes in Season 4 are simply too stiff or sober, proof that the stylish froth of *The Avengers* is just as important as the disturbing, subversive undercurrents. It is when these two are simultaneously present, battling for supremacy, that the show is at its most revolutionary, innovative, thought-provoking and exciting. Paradoxically, when humour is (almost) taken out of the equation –

The Hour That Never Was, *The House That Jack Built* and *The Joker* – the final product is disturbingly subversive, our desire for 'froth' provided by an eccentric tramp, perhaps, or a bizarre young stranger, rather than witty dialogue.

Of course *The Avengers was* formulaic, with 'teaser', diabolical mastermind, murders, fight scenes and 'tag' all obligatory parts of the structure. Within these boundaries, however, the best episodes are able to surprise, amuse and disturb viewers. We are taken well beyond formula, but within a formulaic structure. Another paradox!

The quality of the scripts, direction, the two leading actors, the original music, the sets and locations are all vital ingredients in the success, both critically and commercially, of Season 4. The individual episodes were treated as short films, rather than simply slices of a series, with music and costumes 'cast' for that specific hour. This made each one distinctive. It is a great shame that, as the series neared the end, music was often recycled from earlier seasons. It is symptomatic of the diminishing variety, as is the reworking of former storylines and the dilution of the female lead's mental and physical prowess. In Season 4 the poor episodes stand out; in Season 5 it is the innovative ones which are, arguably, the exceptions rather than the rule. (The Tara King era would help to redress the balance.)

The continuing interest – including academic and online forums – in the show, and its global popularity, half a century on, are testimony to its unique appeal. Unfortunately, as I suggested in my introduction, the popular media of daytime TV and chat shows tends to dumb down when examining *The Avengers*, preferring to concentrate on the series' glamour – the fashions, fights and farce – rarely exploring the complex recipe which made this a fascinating, groundbreaking television drama. In contrast, academic studies are always in danger of offering (pseudo) intellectual readings which are inventions of the author rather than the show itself. We need to strike a balance between the two, something which I have attempted to offer here.

The Avengers goes beyond genre and resists labelling. The success of episodes such as *The Hour That Never Was* and *Epic* confirm that the series is at its most interesting when it tests the boundaries of its formulaic structure. At its artistic peak in the mid-1960s, it provided an entertaining but sometimes disconcerting experience; an hour that often was…flowing with 'subversive champagne'.

BIBLIOGRAPHY OF WORKS CONSULTED

The Avengers: Digitally Restored Special Edition: The Complete Series 4 (Optimum Classic/Studio Canal, 2010)

The Avengers: Digitally Restored Special Edition: The Complete Series 5 (Optimum Classic/Studio Canal, 2010)

The Avengers Dossier: The Definitive Unauthorised Guide (Paul Cornell, Martin Day and Keith Topping, Virgin: 1998)

The Avengers: A Celebration (Marcus Hearn, Titan Books/Studio Canal, 2010)

Bright Horizons: The Monochrome World of Emma Peel (Amazon, 2014)

Mrs. Peel, We're Needed: The Technicolor World of Emma Peel (Amazon, 2014)

The Avengers Forever! (David K Smith, copyright 1996-2008) theavengers.tv/forever

Le Monde des Avengers (*theavengers.fr*)

SEASON 4 PRODUCTION ORDER

December 1964-March 1966

The Town of No Return *

The Murder Market

The Master Minds

Dial A Deadly Number

Death at Bargain Prices

Too Many Christmas Trees

The Cybernauts

The Gravediggers

Room Without A View

A Surfeit of H$_2$0

Two's a Crowd

Man-Eater of Surrey Green

Silent Dust

The Hour That Never Was

Castle De'ath

PRODUCTION ORDER (continued)

December 1964-March 1966

The Thirteenth Hole

Small Game for Big Hunters

The Girl from Auntie

Quick-Quick Slow Death

The Danger Makers

A Touch of Brimstone

What the Butler Saw

The House That Jack Built

A Sense of History

How to Succeed…At Murder

Honey for the Prince

(* Filmed first, but later re-filmed with Diana Rigg)

SEASON 5 PRODUCTION ORDER

September 1966-September 1967

The Fear Merchants

Escape in Time

The Bird Who Knew Too Much

From Venus with Love

The See-Through Man

The Winged Avenger

The Living Dead

The Hidden Tiger

The Correct Way to Kill

Never, Never Say Die

Epic

The Superlative Seven

A Funny Thing Happened on the Way to the Station

Something Nasty in the Nursery

The Joker

PRODUCTION ORDER (continued)

September 1966-September 1967

Who's Who???

Death's Door

Return of the Cybernauts

Dead Man's Treasure

The £50,000 Breakfast

You Have Just Been Murdered

Murdersville

The Positive Negative Man

Mission...Highly Improbable

A SURFEIT OF QUESTIONS/A PAUCITY OF ANSWERS

In June 2014 I managed to track down Colin Finbow, the script writer of *A Surfeit of H2O*. My e-mail to him on the evening of Tuesday 10th June was titled 'A surfeit of questions'; he kindly wrote back the following day, under 'A paucity of answers':

I know that many people share my belief that *A Surfeit of H2O* is one of the highlights of the monochrome filmed season. Lots of location shooting, the bizarre deaths by drowning in fields which are normally dry – Suffolk? – the odd assortment of biblically named locals and the diabolical mastermind with his deadly wine press. What gave you the idea for this episode? It is one which seems to share a similar ecological theme as my father's *Silent Dust*: i.e. science destroying nature.

I've always been sympathetic to the science v nature theme and (before all the hype about climate change) imagined what would happen if science developed a reliable way to create rain. Like so many of our inventions for good, someone would surely use it for evil ends. The mad scientist and the Noah supporters came along with the basic notion! (I understand the 1998 movie version used this premise. Someone sent me a script to read, but it didn't seem to have any of the TV 'Avengers' qualities. I never saw the film.)

How did you come to be asked to write for the show?

My agent Peggy Ramsay told me someone was interested and followed it up. I don't remember any details.

Were you happy with the finished episode?

It looked like a regular 'Avengers' episode. I was chuffed.

Was the Mini-Moke your idea?

Sadly not. I knew (know) nothing about cars, so Brian Clemens, who owned the only E Type Jaguar I have ever ridden in must have been the inspiration here.

Were you aware of the show before you were invited on board?

Yes, an ardent fan ever since the Ian Hendry days. It had the qualities of my own radio and TV writing, so I was delighted to get the chance to contribute. (I had another idea about an eccentric scientist living in a submarine and sending radio signals which could only be received by Walkman headphones. His aim to subjugate the nation's youth by radio hypnosis and cause a civil war to wipe out earth's population for him to reclaim it as his dry domain. I didn't get around to writing it, or pitching it.)

What do you think made it the cult success worldwide which it became and why is it still so popular?

Its quirkiness and blend of humour and suspense, although never universally popular, will always have a place in our culture. I collect a great deal of world cinema, largely because quirkiness and eccentricity are more common in their films and the routine and dumbed down current fare in UK and US largely leaves me cold.

June 2014

Online debate with fellow Avengers can be found at:

avengersfanforum.s2.bizhat.com

Any questions, feedback or criticism about this book will be welcomed and can be directed to me at:

rodneymarshall628@btinternet.com

Printed in Poland
by Amazon Fulfillment
Poland Sp. z o.o., Wrocław